Tartarian
Lady.

A Maid
Servant.

A Bonzess.

A Country
Woman.

Mandarins
Chinese.

of War,
Tartarian.

A
Bonze

A
Country Man

SINOPHILES AND SINOPHOBES
WESTERN VIEWS OF CHINA

LITERARY ANTHOLOGIES OF ASIA

China's Treaty Ports:
Half Love and Half Hate
CHRIS ELDER

Chinese Ink, Western Pen:
Stories of China
BARBARA BAKER

Hong Kong:
Somewhere Between Heaven and Earth
BARBARA-SUE WHITE

Macao:
Mysterious Decay and Romance
DONALD PITTIS & SUSAN J. HENDERS

Old Peking:
City of the Ruler of the World
CHRIS ELDER

Shanghai:
Electric and Lurid City
BARBARA BAKER

Sinophiles and Sinophobes:
Western Views of China
COLIN MACKERRAS

Yangtze River:
The Wildest, Wickedest River on Earth
MADELEINE LYNN

Sinophiles and Sinophobes
Western Views of China

AN ANTHOLOGY SELECTED AND EDITED
BY

Colin Mackerras

OXFORD
UNIVERSITY PRESS

OXFORD
UNIVERSITY PRESS

Oxford University Press is a department of the University of Oxford.
It furthers the University's objective of excellence in research, scholarship,
and education by publishing worldwide in

Oxford New York

Athens Auckland Bangkok Bogotá Buenos Aires Calcutta
Cape Town Chennai Dar es Salaam Delhi Florence Hong Kong Istanbul
Karachi Kuala Lumpur Madrid Melbourne Mexico City Mumbai
Nairobi Paris São Paulo Shanghai Singapore Taipei Tokyo Toronto Warsaw

with associated companies in Berlin Ibadan

Oxford is a registered trade mark of Oxford University Press

Published in the United States
by Oxford University Press Inc., New York

British Library Cataloguing in Publication Data
available

Library of Congress Cataloging-in-Publication Data
available

ISBN 0-19-591892-4

Printed in Hong Kong
Published by Oxford University Press (China) Ltd
18th Floor, Warwick House East, Taikoo Place, 979 King's Road, Quarry Bay
Hong Kong

ACKNOWLEDGEMENTS

The Editor and Publisher wish to thank the following publishers, authors, and agents for permission to reproduce copyright material:

Richard Baum, *Burying Mao, Chinese Politics in the Age of Deng Xiaoping*, copyright © 1994 by Princeton University Press. Reprinted by permission of Princeton University Press; Reproduced, with permission, from Caroline Blunden and Mark Elvin, *The Cultural Atlas of the World, China*, Andromeda, Oxford, Stonehenge, Alexandria, Va., 1990 © authors; Reproduced, with permission, from Richard Bernstein, *From the Center of the Earth* © 1982, Little, Brown, New York; Reproduced, with permission, from C. R. Boxer, ed., *South China in the Sixteenth Century, Being the Narratives of Galeote Pereira, Fr. Gaspar da Cruz, O.P., Fr. Martín de Rada, O.E.S.A. (1559–1575)*, Hakluyt Society, London, 1953 © David Higham Associates; From Fox Butterfield, *China, Alive in the Bitter Sea*, Reproduced by permission of Random House and Hodder and Stoughton Limited Copyright © 1982 by Fox Butterfield; From *China in the Sixteenth Century: The Journals of Matthew Ricci: 1583–1610*, translated by Louis J. Gallagher, SJ Copyright © 1953 by Louis J. Gallagher, SJ. Reprinted by permission of Random House, Inc.; From *People's China: A Brief History, Third Edition* by Craig Dietrich. Copyright © 1986, 1994, 1998 by Oxford University Press, Inc. Used by permission of Oxford University Press, Inc.; From Fredric M. Kaplan, a.o., *Encyclopedia of China Today*, reproduced with permission Fredric M. Kaplan, editor and publisher, Eurasia Press, Inc.; From *China Wakes* by Nicholas D. Kristof and Sheryl WuDunn. Copyright © 1994 by Nicholas Kristof and Sheryl WuDunn. Reprinted by permission of Times Books, a division of Random House, Inc.; Reproduced, with permission, from Alasdair Clayre, *The Heart of the Dragon*, Collins/Harvill, London, 1984 © Harvill Press; Reproduced from Cradock, Percy, *Experiences of China*, John Murray, London, 1994 with permission of John Murray; Reproduced from *An Embassy to China*, edited by J. L. Cranmer-Byng, Longmans, Green and Co., London, 1962, with permission of Pearson Education Limited, Harlow,

Essex; From *China Rising*, copyright © 1990 by Lee Feigon, by permission of Ivan R. Dee, Inc.; Reprinted by permission of Stephen FitzGerald, *Is Australia an Asian Country?*, Allen & Unwin, Sydney, 1997 © Stephen FitzGerald; Reproduced from Rodney Gilbert, *What's Wrong with China*, John Murray, London, 1926, with permission of John Murray; Reproduced, with permission, from Eric Gordon, *Freedom Is a Word*, Hodder and Stoughton, London, 1971 © Eric Gordon; Reproduced, with permission, from Hicks, George, ed., *The Broken Mirror: China After Tiananmen*, Longman Current Affairs, London, 1990 © Financial Times Business; Reproduced, with permission, from *The China Handbook*, edited by Christopher Hudson, Chicago and London: Fitzroy Dearborn Publishers, 1997; Reproduced, with the permission of the University of Michigan Press, *The Legacy of Tiananmen, China in Disarray*, by James A. R. Miles, the University of Michigan Press, Ann Arbor, 1996; Reproduced, with the permission of the Cambridge University Press, Montesquieu, translated and edited by Anne M. Cohler, Basia Carolyn Miller, and Harold Samuel Stone, *The Spirit of the Laws*, Cambridge University Press, Cambridge, 1989; From *China's Crisis, Dilemmas of Reform and Prospects for Democracy*, by Andrew J. Nathan, copyright © 1990 Columbia University Press. Reprinted with the permission of the publisher; Copyright © 1992 by *The New York Times*. Reprinted by permission; Copyright © 1995 by *The New York Times*. Reprinted by permission; Reproduced, with permission, from Michel C. Oksenberg, Michael D. Swaine, and Daniel C. Lynch, *The Chinese Future*, Pacific Council on International Policy, Los Angeles, and Rand Center for Asia-Pacific Policy, Santa Monica, California, 1997; Reproduced with the permission of HarperCollins Publishers, Harrison E. Salisbury, *The New Emperors, China in the Era of Mao and Deng*, Little, Brown, 1992; Reproduced with the permission of the publisher, Agnes Smedley, *China's Red Army Marches*, Lawrence and Wishart, London, 1936; Reproduced by permission of Grove/Atlantic, Inc. from Edgar Snow, *Red Star Over China*, first revised and enlarged edition, Grove Press, New York, 1968; Reproduced by permission of Lonely Planet Publications from Chris Taylor, Robert Storey, Nicko Goncharoff, a.o., *China A Lonely Planet Travel Survival Kit*, fifth edition, Lonely Planet Publications, Melbourne, Oakland, CA, London, Paris, 1996; Reproduced from Arnold J. Toynbee, *A Journey to China or Things*

Which Are Seen, Constable, London, 1931, with permission; Reproduced from *The Chinese People Stand Up* by Elizabeth Wright, with permission of BBC Worldwide Limited © Elizabeth Wright, 1989; Reproduced, with permission, from Yule, Colonel Sir Henry and Cordier, Henri, *Cathay and the Way Thither, Being a Collection of Medieval Notices of China*, The Hakluyt Society, London, 1915, Vol. II, © David Higham Associates.

Pictures, reprinted with permission, State Library of South Australia, Part III; published with the permission of Joscelyn Burn, Parts VIII and IX (other than the drawings from Carl Crow, drawings by G. Sapojnikoff, *Four Hundred Million Customers*, Hamish Hamilton, London, 1937).

In some cases it has not been possible, despite every effort, to locate those with rights to material possibly still in copyright. The publisher would be glad to hear from anyone who holds such rights, in order that appropriate acknowledgement can be made in any future editions.

Endpapers from J. B. Du Halde, 'The Various Habits of the Chinese and Tartars', *The General History of China*, 1736, Vol II.

PREFACE

This book is presented for all those interested in China, not simply students or government personnel, but also—perhaps primarily—for the interested general reader. The motivation for writing it is fascination with a country that I have studied, visited, and—for all its many faults—come to love over a period of thirty-five years.

I have written a book entitled *Western Images of China*, and the present book refers to some of the same works mentioned there. At the same time, it is a completely different book, since it aims more to bring together interesting and relevant extracts about how Western people have seen China than to analyse or describe their perceptions.

Since the passages range over a very long period, they inevitably use different romanization systems. Nowadays, the system adopted in the People's Republic of China and elsewhere is *pinyin*, but this system was devised only in the 1950s and did not come into general use in the West until the 1980s. To avoid confusion I have, following the first occurrence of the original romanization given in each extract, usually given the name or term in *pinyin* in square brackets.

It is my pleasure to thank all those who have contributed to this volume. They are too numerous to mention personally. They fall into three main categories: the Chinese people themselves, my students and colleagues in the China field, and my family. All have inspired me and not only kept my interest in China alive, but made it more intense over the years since I paid my first visit there in August 1964.

Colin Mackerras
May 2000

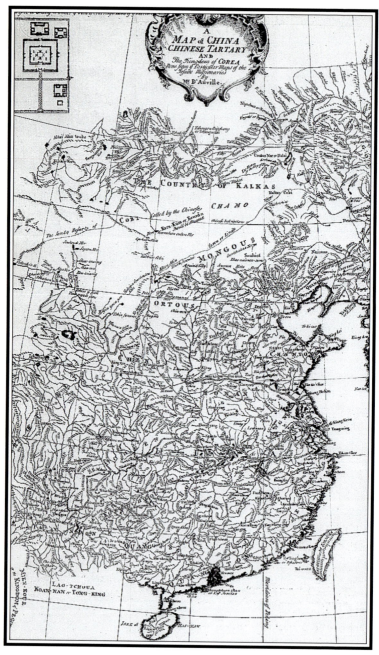

A Map of China, Chinese Tartary, and the Kingdom of Corea. Source: J. B. Du Halde, *The General History of China.*

CONTENTS

CONTENTS

CONTENTS

PART XI: THE PENDULUM SWINGS AGAIN

PART XII: A MODERN BACKLASH

INTRODUCTION

China has long fascinated the West. Yet although Europe has known of China as the producer of silk at least since Roman times, it was not until the sixteenth century that the first major works specifically and exclusively about China appeared in European languages. Marco Polo (*c.* 1254–1324) was long reputed to be the first European to live in China, return to Europe, and write of his experiences. Frances Wood doubts whether Marco Polo ever travelled much further than the Black Sea or Constantinople, arguing instead that his work was based on hearsay. Nevertheless, there is no doubting that Polo's writings remain 'a very rich source' about thirteenth-century China, and especially about Beijing. Also, Marco Polo's book was widely influential in Europe and hence affected Western images of China more deeply than any which preceded it.[1]

The Extracts and their Authors

This book is an anthology of writings by Westerners about China. Its main aims are to present extracts that show salient Western views of China and to arouse interest among general readers concerning these views, past and present. I present some interpretation to accompany the extracts, and in places give historical background. However, this anthology does *not* intend to be a scholarly treatment of Western perceptions of China.

The presentation of the passages is chronological; all are contemporary with the period they describe, written within thirty years of that period. In a few cases, an extract is placed in the chapter appropriate to its content, not to its time of writing. For example, a document written in the 1980s about the 1960s would belong in Part X, not Part XII.

All the extracts here were written not long after what they discuss because images of China's past have their own fascination, just as do those of her present. One thinks of the cruel Chinese princess Turandot in the last opera by Giacomo Puccini (1858–1924), set centuries or millennia before the date of composition in a land where time did not seem to matter and change did not occur. Images of China's past may influence those of her present, but they are definitely a different topic altogether.

Sinophiles and Sinophobes begins with the thirteenth century and ends at the close of the twentieth. The reason for the first time boundary is simply that only in the thirteenth century do 'sinophiles' or 'sinophobes' begin to write more than a few paragraphs about China. In other words, only then do descriptions become detailed enough to be really interesting. The extracts become more copious with the passage of time, and the twentieth century is the best represented of all periods. This book's completion coincided almost exactly with the end of the twentieth century, so it seems natural that this should be the last century represented.

The authors are of varied backgrounds and types: travellers, adventurers, missionaries, clerics, diplomats, journalists, scholars, traders, and businessmen. Those who wrote about China at the beginning of the twentieth century were far more likely to be missionaries than those writing at its end. The profession of journalism is comparatively new, which means that whereas journalists stationed in China were both numerous and prolific in the last decades of the twentieth century, they did not exist at all in the early part of the nineteenth century, let alone in the eighteenth century or before.

With but few exceptions, such as Isabella Lucy Bird (1831–1904), all writers on China before the twentieth century were men. This anthology, however, includes several female writers. The twentieth century saw prominent female writers on China, such as Pearl Buck (1892–1973) and Agnes Smedley (1892–1950), and the second half of the twentieth century witnessed women move into all the professions in the West.

Not all writers about China have actually visited the country. Even in the twentieth century, authors like Arthur Waley (1889–1966) researched and wrote much on China but never went there. Waley is not represented in this volume because he restricted himself to researching and writing about China's past. The list of those who are represented here despite never having set foot in China include some distinguished names. Leaving aside Marco Polo, who most people think did actually visit China, the most important of these is the great eighteenth-century French Jesuit sinologist J. B. Du Halde (1674–1743).

In using the terms 'Western views of China' and 'the West', to which places is this book referring? Initially, the geographical, political, and cultural implications of the term 'the West' corresponded to each other because the western end of the great Eurasian continent and islands off its coast were equivalent to that region which produced 'Western' culture. Later, with the rise of European-based civilizations in America and elsewhere, there was no longer a correspondence between the spatial, political, and cultural concepts of 'the West'.

Even if one restricted coverage to the early centuries, it would be necessary to ask questions about precisely what was meant by 'the West'. Presumably it would include the great states of central Europe (such as the Hapsburg Empire), even though they were actually east of France, Spain, and Britain, since they produced such marvels of 'Western' civilization as the music of Wolfgang Amadeus Mozart and Franz Schubert and supreme examples of 'Western' architecture.

The question of politics and culture also raises the issue of what to include in 'the West'. Presumably Britain, France, Italy, and Germany can count as 'the West' at virtually all times, even though their borders have not been constant throughout history. But was Spain politically part of 'the West' during the centuries when it was dominated by Muslim caliphates? On the other hand, North Africa could legitimately be regarded as part of 'the West' during the period it was part of the Roman Empire. It produced some phenomena which are often regarded as icons of Western civilization, such as St Augustine of Hippo (354–430) and the great library of Alexandria. Czechoslovakia was no doubt part of 'the West', both politically and culturally, when part of the Hapsburg Empire, but possibly not during the years it was dominated by a Marxist–Leninist party. The United States could not be included in the West before its settlement by European peoples even though it has dominated Western images of China for much of the period since then. My point is that 'the West' is a shifting political and cultural phenomenon.

Since 'the West' is extremely large, especially in modern times, it is sensible to impose restrictions. In the present book, I have decided to restrict coverage to Italy, Spain, and Portugal for the period from the thirteenth to the seventeenth centuries, and to Britain, France, and the United States for the eighteenth to the twentieth centuries.

To say that the book restricts itself to Britain, France, and the United States for the eighteenth to the twentieth centuries raises the question of whether to emphasize citizenship or place of publication. Would an Australian publishing his work in the United States be included? My general policy is to require that both the author's citizenship and the place of publication fall into one of the three countries listed above; the reason is to limit the scope of an otherwise very broad subject. However, it is neither sensible nor possible to be too rigid in this matter. People change their citizenship, and their place of residence may not be where they were born. I include authors of particular significance for their views on China even if they are not citizens of Britain, France, or the United States, provided their work is published in at least one of those countries. An example is Pierre Ryckmans (b. 1935). A Belgian who settled in Australia, his influential works were published worldwide, but especially in France and the United States.

And what about Chinese people who publish or write in the West? In the twentieth century, especially in its second half, many works about China published in the West were written by Chinese who left China to live in a Western country. Are their views Western? My answer is no. However, those people of Chinese ethnicity are counted as Western if they were born in the West. In other words, my decision is based on culture, not on race.

It is easier to define the term 'China' than 'the West' because a recognizable state known as China has existed from the thirteenth century to the twentieth century. Even in this case, however, the definition is not absolutely straightforward. After all, the borders of China have changed over these centuries, and regions such as Taiwan and Tibet have at times since the thirteenth century been out of the control of the central government. In this book 'China' designates those territories governed by the People's Republic of China at the end of the twentieth century, apart from Hong Kong and Macao. In practice, there is no entry about Taiwan and few concerning Tibet or other areas of China's far west.

The Western authors presented here wrote about China believing that what they wrote was factual. In other words, I have included no fictional extracts, although there are a few by great fiction writers. It is worth making the point that the extracts are meant as reality, even though the boundary between fiction and fact can often seem blurred. My rule is that what is presented as fiction is excluded, but what is presented as fact can be included.

The factual material covers the following topics:

- social situations;
- individual people;
- groups of people, including women;
- social habits or practices;
- education;
- health;
- political systems;
- ideas, including religion;
- lifestyle;
- economy;
- China's place in the world; and
- evaluations of the situation in China, or its future, which include at least one of the above topics.

Many types of interesting material, such as the arts and sciences, are not included within this purview. Also, the extracts contain little about China's foreign policy or foreign relations. Restrictions for practical purposes are the reason for excluding these subjects.

On the whole, this book is not aimed at the description, discussion, or analysis of major historical events. The extracts avoid the Boxer Uprising of 1900, the fall of the Manchu Dynasty in 1911, the Northern Expedition of 1927–8, the accession to power of the Chinese Communist Party in 1949, and the June 4 Incident of 1989. However, some entries take up topics, as noted above, that fall within the periods of such major events, and the inclusion of 'individual people' allows the coverage of historical figures.

As will be noted in the next section, views of China tend to take up a generally favourable or hostile attitude towards their subject. It has proved very difficult for writers to remain totally dispassionate or neutral. Even passages that appear to be merely descriptive are likely to choose facts which illustrate one point of view or another. In the following passages, there is some commentary on the authors, who they were and their points of view, and the overall attitudes which people of a particular period adopted. However, I should emphasize that the extracts are not chosen to represent a particular point of view.

Summary of Western Views of China

Whether Marco Polo in fact visited China or not, much of his book concerns China, and thus commences the first great age of 'Sinophiles and Sinophobes'. Polo was extremely positive about China, writing in glowing terms of its governance and cities, notably Beijing and Hangzhou. Above all, he describes China as a land of great prosperity and flourishing commerce and claims that the emperor took a personal interest in the well-being of his subjects. Because of his account, north China, or Cathay, became famous for over two centuries as synonymous with El Dorado, 'a fabulous land of wealth on the far side of the world'.[2]

In the fourteenth century also, the popes were sending clerics east to the Mongol court to try to enlist its support against Islam, and missionaries went to China to convert the people to Christianity. They tended strongly to confirm and continue the enthusiastic view of Marco Polo. By far the most important was Odoric of Pordenone (c. 1286–1331), who lived in China during the 1320s. The first Western observer to write of the custom of foot-binding, he remained extremely positive about China and was greatly impressed by the magnificent cities he saw. Shortly after Odoric's visit, contacts between China and Europe were cut off, among other factors by the great plague epidemic in Europe, known as the Black Death, which killed about one-third of its population between 1348 and 1351. The first great age of 'Western views of China' was over.

The next age was roughly the second half of the sixteenth century, 'the century of discovery'. Although this age was initially mostly concerned with Asian countries other than China, it saw the publication of the first great compendia about that country, especially Juan Gonzalez de Mendoza's *History of the Great and Mighty Kingdom of China*, published in Spanish in Rome in 1585. Dominated by the Spaniards and Portuguese, the Western writers of the sixteenth century were also positive about China, though somewhat less so than during the 'first great age'.

This second age fused with the third period, which focuses on the work of the priests of the Society of Jesus, or Jesuits. The contribution that the Jesuits, especially those of France, made to the history of sinology remains of enormous importance. At the head of this line of Jesuit missionaries and scholars stood the

Italian Matteo Ricci, who actually lived in the Chinese capital of Beijing in the first decade of the seventeenth century, dying there in 1610. This age saw works of great sinologists like J. B. Du Halde, who influenced a range of important thinkers, especially Voltaire (1694–1778), towards a positive view of China. Although the Jesuit writers and Voltaire were also extremely positive about China, this period was much more complicated than the ones which preceded it, with titanic political struggles and theological debates being fought over issues involving the nature of China and its government and society. Many did not share the enthusiasm of the Society of Jesus, notably the Dominicans; the Papacy adopted this latter view, ultimately suppressing the Jesuits in 1773.

In the second half of the eighteenth century, the trend moved away from the dominantly positive view that had characterized this third great age to a fourth, decisively more negative period, which lasted until the beginning of the twentieth century. This fourth age saw the Industrial Revolution in Britain and elsewhere. A sense of confidence and nationalism resulted in imperialist approaches to China and much of the rest of the world. The dominant countries of this period were Britain and France, with the United States asserting itself as a major player from about the middle of the nineteenth century, especially with the publication in 1848 of Samuel Wells Williams's (1812–84) magisterial *The Middle Kingdom*. This negative age featured missionaries, diplomats, scholars, and adventurers among those whose Western perspectives contributed to the views held in their countries about China. These people formed a wider range of observers than had existed in earlier centuries. The climax of this fourth, negative age came with the Boxer Uprising in 1900.

The first fifty years of the twentieth century can be taken as the fifth age of Western views of China. In China, this century saw the fall of the Manchu (Qing) Dynasty in 1911, the rise of the Nationalist Party under Chiang Kai-shek (1887–1975) in 1927, and the War of Resistance Against Japan, which lasted from 1937 to 1945. Finally, it saw the victory of the Chinese Communist Party (CCP) over the Nationalists and Chiang Kai-shek in 1949. In terms of Western images, it saw a much more positive view of China, an attitude which became more enthusiastic when China became an ally of the West during World War II. It was above all in the United States that this view prevailed, and it was there that the media work of the strongly pro-Chiang Kai-shek Henry Luce (1898–1967), based on the widely read periodical *Time*, had its greatest influence. Luce was born into a missionary family in China and was a passionate supporter of missionary work. In the first half of the twentieth century, the United States established itself as the most important Western country to engage and view China, a dominance which increased in the second half and looks set to persist into the twenty-first century.

In Europe, Britain and France also produced missionaries, scholars, diplomats, and others who wrote on China. Their perceptions also underwent a clear movement towards a positive view of China. Europe, however, seems to have retained a more vociferously hostile, even racist camp than existed in the United States, probably due to the continuing impact of colonialist thinking.

The sixth period of Western views of China spans from 1949 to 1972 and, apart from his last four years, coincides with the rule of Mao Zedong (1893–1976). During this period, Western views of China were generally very negative indeed. This was the height of the Cold War, when Westerners tended strongly to view countries ruled by communist parties as oppressed and unfortunate, and communism as a wrong, even evil ideology. The height of the totalitarian era was the Cultural Revolution of the late 1960s, when a Chinese government curtailed the freedom of its own people more savagely than at any other time in the twentieth century.

At the same time, this sixth period also saw a group of Westerners prepared to sympathize with the People's Republic of China and even with its government. This counter-trend gathered momentum in the 1960s because it was associated with opposition to American military intervention in Vietnam aimed at suppressing a leftist revolution there.

In February 1972, United States President Richard Nixon, who had been a major advocate of America's military effort in Vietnam, actually visited China for a week and met the dictator Mao Zedong. This visit gave a major boost to the cause of those who had been prepared to see some good in Communist China and led on to the seventh period of 'Sinophiles and Sinophobes'. This period was distinctly more positive than its predecessor. Once again, Westerners not only visited China but actually lived there in numbers far greater than had been the case since the 1950s. Most

Western countries established diplomatic relations with China in the early 1970s, and the United States followed suit at the beginning of 1979. The period of positive images was also one in which, on the whole, relations between China and the West improved greatly.

The last, or eighth, main period of Western views of China dates from the middle of 1989. At that time, the Chinese government suppressed a large-scale student movement by moving tanks and other armoured vehicles into the centre of Beijing. The result was a violent incident which killed a number of people in the capital, in front of many Western observers. The impact of this incident on Western views of China was profound. It led to a period of restraint during which most Western countries placed far more emphasis on human rights and China's shortcomings in this area.

During the 1990s, China's economic performance improved. Its ability to withstand the worst effects of the economic crisis which swept most of East and South-East Asia from the middle of 1997 won China great credit from Western governments and observers. However, this was balanced by a rather critical view of China's government and social development. The view of the West was more complicated and mixed during the last decade of the twentieth century than it had been before. It can be summed up as follows: 'Economic performance, very good, human rights, poor, not a very nice place, really'. Diplomatically, China's relations with Western countries generally improved. The Cold War was no more, though China stood out as one of the last remaining states still ruled by a communist party.

Ideas on Western Views of China

Studies have noted the existence of a pendulum between positive and negative images of China, an excellent example being the shift from the highly laudatory views pushed by the Jesuit writers in the seventeenth and first part of the eighteenth century, to the extremely negative views predominant in the nineteenth century. A caution needs to be raised, however, about this theory; it is in no sense absolute or exclusive. Views opposite to the dominant trend may coexist with the more fashionable and prevailing views, and in a particular Western country, different views may be found in greater profusion than in another. Yet this relativist position does not seem to undermine the validity of the pendulum theory of Western views of China.[3]

The periods of positive and negative views normally blend into each other. There are cases, however, where the opposite is true. One specific example is the break occasioned by the visit of Richard Nixon to China in February 1972, which swung the pendulum quickly from negative to positive. A swing in the opposite direction became very evident when the Chinese government suppressed the student movement in early June 1989.

The periods of positive and negative are sometimes unclear and may vary greatly in length. On the whole, the more recent the period of favourable or unfavourable views, the shorter it is likely to be. The positive period following Nixon's visit lasted less than two decades. In contrast, the era of negative views which focused on the nineteenth century lasted well over 100 years.

The dominant images of a period seem to accord roughly with the interests of the main Western countries of the day. In the 1950s and 1960s, the West saw Communist China as a dangerous, aggressive enemy, and thus the dominant images were extremely negative. But correspondingly, the desire to bring China into the world forum of nations in the early 1970s saw a rapid and thorough swing in images from negative to positive.

As with the 'pendulum' theory, this idea that power within societies influences views on other countries cannot be interpreted as absolute, because there are exceptions and complexities. Moreover, the theory carries no implication of any political conspiracies influencing the way people in the West see China. The fact that there are so often views alternative to the dominant ones is ample proof that Western societies have virtually always been able to generate a range of perceptions on all issues, including those of moment concerning other civilizations. But it nevertheless remains true that Western views of China have political overtones and implications, even when they appear to be entirely neutral. The extracts in this book should make this clear.

PART I

EARLY ADVENTURES

What matters about Marco Polo is not whether he actually visited China but that he left an account of it which has become famous throughout the world. He can claim to have been the first Westerner to leave a detailed record about China, one which, with exceptions, accords with what we know from other sources. It justly occupies an important place in the history of 'Sinophiles and Sinophobes'.

Marco Polo claimed to have lived and travelled in China for some seventeen years. After his return to Italy he was a naval officer and became a prisoner of war during the years 1298–99; at this time he dictated his claimed experiences to a fellow prisoner, Rustichello of Pisa. Marco Polo's account became popular immediately and the major part of it entered the literature of the period.

1
THE WONDERS OF KIN-SAI

MARCO POLO

TRANSLATED BY WILLIAM MARSDEN

In the following extracts Marco Polo comments on the city he calls Kin-sai. It had been the capital of the just-conquered China of the Southern Song dynasty (1126–79), which he calls Manji, and is in the same location as present-day Hangzhou, capital of Zhejiang Province. Under the Mongols, whose emperor Marco Polo called the grand khan, Kin-sai remained a great city and much impressed Marco Polo for its size and splendour and for the variety and prosperity of its food economy.

Of the Noble and Magnificent City of Kin-sai

At the end of three days you reach the noble and magnificent city of Kin-sai, a name that signifies 'the celestial city,' and which it merits from its preeminence to all others in the world, in point of grandeur and beauty, as well as from its abundant delights, which might lead an inhabitant to imagine himself in paradise. . . . According to common estimation, this city is a hundred miles in circuit. Its streets and canals are extensive, and there are squares, or marketplaces, which, being necessarily proportioned in size to the prodigious concourse of people by whom they are frequented, are exceedingly spacious. It is situated between a lake of fresh and very clear water on the one side, and a river of great magnitude on the other, the waters of which, by a number of canals, large and small, are made to run through every quarter of the city, carrying with them all the filth into the lake, and ultimately to the sea. This, whilst it contributes much to the purity of the air, furnishes a communication by water, in addition to that by land, to all parts of the town; the canals and the streets being of sufficient width to allow of boats on the one, and carriages in the other, conveniently

3

passing, with articles necessary for the consumption of the inhabitants. It is commonly said that the number of bridges, of all sizes, amounts to twelve thousand. Those which are thrown over the principal canals and are connected with the main streets, have arches so high, and built with so much skill, that vessels with their masts can pass under them, whilst, at the same time, carts and horses are passing over their heads, so well is the slope from the street adapted to the height of the arch. If they were not in fact so numerous, there would be no convenience of crossing from one place to another. . . .

There are within the city ten principal squares or marketplaces, besides innumerable shops along the streets. Each side of these squares is half a mile in length, and in front of them is the main street, forty paces in width, and running in a direct line from one extremity of the city to the other. It is crossed by many low and convenient bridges. These market-squares (two miles in their whole dimension) are at the distance of four miles from each other. In a direction parallel to that of the main street, but on the opposite side of the squares, runs a very large canal, on the nearer bank of which capacious warehouses are built of stone, for the accommodation of the merchants who arrive from India and other parts, together with their goods and effects, in order that they may be conveniently situated with respect to the marketplaces. In each of these, upon three days in every week, there is an assemblage of from forty to fifty thousand persons, who attend the markets and supply them with every article of provision that can be desired. There is an abundant quantity of game of all kinds, such as roebucks, stags, fallow deer, hares, and rabbits, together with partridges, pheasants, francolins, quails, common fowls, capons, and such numbers of ducks and geese as can scarcely be expressed; for so easily are they bred and reared on the lake, that, for the value of a Venetian silver groat, you may purchase a couple of geese and two couple of ducks. There, also, are the shambles, where they slaughter cattle for food, such as oxen, calves, kids, and lambs, to furnish the tables of rich persons and of the great magistrates. As to people of the lower classes, they do not scruple to eat every other kind of flesh, however unclean, without any discrimination. At all seasons there is in the markets a great variety of herbs and fruits, and especially pears of an extraordinary size, weighing ten pounds each, that are white in the inside, like paste, and have a very

THE WONDERS OF KIN-SAI

fragrant smell. There are peaches also, in their season, both of the yellow and the white kinds, and of a delicious flavour. Grapes are not produced there, but are brought in a dried state, and very good, from other parts. This applies also to wine, which the natives do not hold in estimation, being accustomed to their own liquor prepared from rice and spices. From the sea, which is fifteen miles distant, there is daily brought up the river, to the city, a vast quantity of fish; and in the lake also there is abundance, which gives employment at all times to persons whose sole occupation is to catch them.

Marco Polo claims to have visited the city of Kin-sai many times. He was most impressed with several of its social aspects, which he describes below.

The streets connected with the market-squares are so numerous, and in some of them are many cold baths, attended by servants of both sexes, to perform the offices of ablution for the men and women who frequent them, and who from their childhood have been accustomed at all times to wash in cold water, which they reckon highly conducive to health. At these bathing places, however, they have apartments provided with warm water, for the use of strangers, who, from not being habituated to it, cannot bear the shock of the cold. All are in the daily practice of washing their persons, and especially before their meals.

In other streets are the habitations of the courtesans, who are here in such numbers as I dare not venture to report: and not only near the squares, which is the situation usually appropriated for their residence, but in every part of the city they are to be found, adorned with much finery, highly perfumed, occupying well-furnished houses, and attended by many female domestics. These women are accomplished, and are perfect in the arts of blandishment and dalliance, which they accompany with expressions adapted to every description of person, insomuch that strangers who have once tasted of their charms, remain in a state of fascination, and become so enchanted by their meretricious arts that they can never divest themselves of the impression. Thus intoxicated with sensual pleasures, when they return to their homes they report that they have been in Kin-sai, or the celestial city, and pant for the time when they may be enabled to revisit paradise. In other streets are the dwellings of the physicians and the astrologers, who also give instructions in reading and writing, as well as in many other arts. They have apartments also amongst those which surround the market-squares. On opposite sides of each of these squares there are two large edifices, where officers appointed by the grand khan are stationed, to take immediate cognisance of any differences that may happen to arise between the foreign merchants, or amongst the inhabitants of the place.

Marco Polo continues with a discussion of the economy and occupations of the people. He then comments on their nature, especially their friendliness and love of peace. In retrospect this is ironical, considering the fear of China which prevailed in later centuries. There is a sting in the tail of this passage, for it is obvious that Marco Polo was aware of the resentment the Chinese felt at being under Mongol domination.

The inhabitants of the city are idolaters, and they use paper money as currency. The men as well as the women have fair complexions, and are handsome. The greater part of them are always clothed in silk, in consequence of the vast quantity of that material produced in the territory of Kin-sai, exclusively of what the merchants import from other provinces. Amongst the handicraft trades exercised in the place, there are twelve considered to be superior to the rest, as being more generally useful; for each of which there are a thousand workshops, and each shop furnishes employment for ten, fifteen, or twenty workmen, and in a few instances as many as forty, under their respective masters. The opulent principals in these manufactories do not labour with their own hands, but, on the contrary, assume airs of gentility and affect parade. Their wives equally abstain from work. They have much beauty, as has been remarked, and are brought up with delicate and languid habits. The costliness of their dresses, in silks and jewellery, can scarcely be imagined. Although the laws of their ancient kings ordained that each citizen should exercise the profession of his father, yet they were allowed, when they acquired wealth, to discontinue the manual labour, provided they kept up the establishment, and

6

employed persons to work at their paternal trades. Their houses are well built and richly adorned with carved work. So much do they delight in ornaments of this kind, in paintings, and fancy buildings, that the sums they lavish on such objects are enormous. The natural disposition of the native inhabitants of Kin-sai is pacific, and by the example of their former kings, who were themselves unwarlike, they have been accustomed to habits of tranquillity. The management of arms is unknown to them, nor do they keep any in their houses. Contentious broils are never heard among them. They conduct their mercantile and manufacturing concerns with perfect candour and probity. They are friendly towards each other, and persons who inhabit the same street, both men and women, from the mere circumstances of neighbourhood, appear like one family. In their domestic manners they are free from jealousy or suspicion of their wives, to whom great respect is shown, and any man would be accounted infamous who should presume to use indecent expressions to a married woman. To strangers also, who visit their city in the way of commerce, they give proofs of cordiality, inviting them freely to their houses, showing them hospitable attention, and furnishing them with the best advice and assistance in their mercantile transactions. On the other hand, they dislike the sight of soldiery, not excepting the guards of the grand khan, as they preserve the recollection that by them they were deprived of the government of their native kings and rulers.

2

ODORIC ARGUES WITH A BUDDHIST

ODORIC OF PORDENONE

TRANSLATED BY SIR HENRY YULE

Among the fourteenth-century travellers to China, the most famous and influential was Odoric of Pordenone. Odoric was a Franciscan friar, keen to convert as well as observe. He attacks 'idolators' (Buddhists), yet it is striking how enthusiastic he remained about China. He stayed there for about three years.

Odoric comments that Hangzhou, which he calls Cansai, is 'the greatest city in the whole world' and notes that the city was so great that he would hardly have dared to 'tell of it' except that he had met many people in Venice who had been there. This suggests that quite a few people in fourteenth-century Europe had visited China. He calls the former Southern Song China simply Manzi, obviously a variant of the Manji of Marco Polo.

In the following extract, Odoric describes an argument he had with a Buddhist in a magnificent monastery in Hangzhou. The tone is actually quite positive; Odoric is at pains to let the Buddhist have his say.

The edition used is that of Sir Henry Yule (1820–89) and Henri Cordier (1849–1925). Yule is famous for his immense contribution to the study of Western travel in Asia.

Of the marvellous sight that Friar Odoric beheld in a certain monastery of the idolaters.

This is the royal city in which the king of Manzi formerly dwelt. And four of our friars that were in that city had converted a man that was in authority there, in whose house I was entertained. And he said to me one day: '*Atha* (which is to say *Father*) wilt thou come and see the place?' And when I said that I would willingly go, we got into a boat, and went to a certain great monastery of the people of the country. . . . And he called to him one of their monks, saying: 'Seest here this *Franki Rabban*? (which meaneth this Frank monk). He cometh from where the sun sets, and goeth now to Cambalech [Beijing] to pray for the life of the great Khan. Show him therefore, prithee, something worth seeing, so that if he get back to his own country he may be able to say, I have seen such and such strange things in Cansai!' And the monk replied that he would do so with pleasure.

So he took two great buckets full of scraps from the table, and opening the door of a certain shrubbery which was there we went therein. Now in this shrubbery there is a little hill covered with pleasant trees. . . . And as we stood there he took a gong, and began to beat upon it, and at the sound a multitude of animals of divers kinds began to come down from the hill, such as apes, monkeys, and many other animals having faces like men, to the number of some three thousand, and took up their places round about him in regular ranks. And when they were thus ranged about him, he put down the vessels before them and fed them as fast as he was able. And when they had been fed he began again to beat the gong, and all returned to their retreats. So I, laughing heartily, began to say: 'Tell me, prithee, what this meaneth?' And he answered: 'These animals be the souls of gentlemen, which we feed in this fashion for the love of God!' But quoth I: 'No souls be these, but brute beasts of sundry kinds.' And he said: 'No, forsooth, they be nought else but the souls of gentlemen. For if a man be noble his soul entereth the form of some one of these noble animals; but the souls of boors enter the forms of baser animals and dwell there!' And say what I list against it, nought else would he believe.

But if anyone should desire to tell all the vastness and great marvels of this city, a good quire of stationery would not hold the matter I trow. For 'tis the greatest and noblest city, and the finest for merchandise, that the whole world containeth.

PART II

A CENTURY OF DISCOVERY

W hen Western interest in China revived following the Black Death in the middle of the fourteenth century, it was led by the Iberians. In 1508, the Portuguese King Manuel I sent an expedition to explore Malacca and instructed its leader to enquire about China. Yet it was not until 1557 that the Portuguese secured a firm base in China at the port of Macao, and only later did eyewitness accounts of China by Westerners again reach Europe.

Three Iberians visited China in the second half of the sixteenth century and wrote of their experiences: Galeote Pereira, a Portuguese soldier, sailor and merchant adventurer; Gaspar da Cruz, a Portuguese Dominican priest; and Martín de Rada, a Spanish Augustinian priest.

Da Cruz became the author of the first book in any European language devoted more or less entirely to China. Published in 1569–70, it remained fairly rare and, because it was written in Portuguese, it did not attain great fame outside his own country.

Da Cruz spent only a few months in China and based his writing to a considerable extent on Pereira, frankly acknowledging the debt. His account of China is reasonably comprehensive, encompassing its economy, clothing and customs, and religion. He is generally positive about China, regarding it as prosperous and well governed. His chapter on 'justice', however, gives an exceedingly grim picture of the cruelty of the Chinese legal system.

3

KNAVISH PRIESTS

GASPAR DA CRUZ

TRANSLATED BY C. R. BOXER

The following extracts reveal that the Chinese are subject to few taxes, are industrious, and have no time for lazy people; the blind and disabled are well looked after; and the bureaucracy and people have absolutely no time for the Buddhist and Daoist clergy. As a Catholic priest, Gaspar da Cruz appears to have mixed feelings about this last point. He regarded the clergy as idolaters and therefore viewed them as untrustworthy and deceitful, but was nonetheless surprised at the contempt in which the bureaucracy and people held the clergy, which was in marked contrast to attitudes in his own country.

Of the husbandry of the land and the occupations of the people

China is almost all a well husbanded country; for as the country is well inhabited, and people in abundance, and the men spenders, and using themselves very deliciously in eating and drinking and apparel, and in the other services of their houses, especially that they are great eaters, every one laboureth to get a living, and every one seeketh ways to earn their food, and how to maintain their great expenses. A great help to this is that idle people be much abhorred in this country, and are very odious unto the rest, and he that laboureth not shall not eat, for commonly there is none that do give alms to the poor; wherefore, if any poor man did ask alms of a Portugal, and he did give it to him, the Chinas did laugh at him and asked him mockingly, 'Why givest thou alms to this which is a knave? Let him go and earn it.'

Only some jesters have some reward, standing on some high place where they gather the people around them and tell them some fables to get something. The fathers and priests of their idols are commonly abhorred and not esteemed, because they hold them for idle people, and the magistrates for any light fault do not spare them but give them many stripes. Wherefore, a magistrate whipping once before a Portugal a priest of theirs, and he asking him wherefore he did use their priests so ill and held them in so little esteem, answered him, 'These are idle and abandoned knaves.'

One day, I and certain Portugals entering into the house of the Comptroller of the Revenue, about the delivery of certain Portugals that were in prison, because the matter belongs to him for the great profit that came thereof to the King, much people came in with us to see us, among the which there was a priest; as soon as the magistrate said, 'Set them down,' all of them ran away in great haste, the priest running as all the rest, for fear of the whip. . . .

Every one laboureth to seek a living, for that which he earneth he enjoyeth freely, and spends it as he will, and that which is left him at his death remains to his children and grandchildren, paying only duties royal, as well of the fruits that they gather, as of the good they deal in, which are not heavy. . . .

I said above that they did not give alms to the poor in this country, and forasmuch as some readers might ask what remedy had the poor who could not earn their bread, through being maimed, crippled, or blind, I thought it good to satisfy them. It is a thing worth noting that the blind have a labour appointed them for to get their food, which is to serve in a horse-mill, like horses grinding corn; and commonly where there is one horse-mill there are two, because one blind man going in each mill, they may recreate themselves in talking one with the other, as I saw them treading the wheel with fans in their hands, fanning themselves and talking very friendly.

The blind women are the common women [prostitutes], and they have nurses that do dress them and paint them with vermillion and ceruse, and receive the wages of their evil use. The lame and the cripple, which either have no kindred within a certain degree, or if they have them and they do not provide for them that which is necessary, or are not able to help them, they make their petition to the Comptroller of the King's Revenue; and their kindred being examined by his officers, if among them are any that can maintain them, they do bind the nearest to take them to their charge and maintain them; and if their kindred be not able to maintain them, or if they have no kindred in the country, the Comptroller of the Revenue commandeth they be received into the King's Hospital; for the King hath in all the cities great hospitals which have many lodgings within a great enclosure. And the officers of the hospital are bound to administer to those that are bed-ridden all things necessary, for the which there are very sufficient rents appointed out of the King's exchequer.

The lame that keep not their bed, have every month a certain quantity of rice, with the which, and with a little hen or a little pig which they bring up in the hospital, they have sufficient to maintain themselves; and all these things are very well paid, without fail. And because commonly those who are received into these hospitals are incurable, they receive them for life. And all those who are received by commandment of the Comptroller of the Revenue are enrolled, and every year the officers of the hospital do yield account of the expenses, and of the provision for the poor and sick; and if any fault of negligence be found in them of that which they are bound to do, without remission they are well punished for it.

4

A WELL-RUN AND PROSPEROUS LAND

JUAN GONZALEZ DE MENDOZA

TRANSLATED BY ROBERT PARKE

The first attempt to collect together in one work all that the West knew about China was Juan Gonzalez de Mendoza's The History of the Great and Mighty Kingdom of China, *published in Spanish in 1585. Mendoza's work was based on the accounts of Galeote Pereira, Gaspar da Cruz, and Martín de Rada, as well as on a range of other material. However, according to C. R. Boxer, Mendoza's account favoured the more positive view of China over that put forward by the Spaniard de Rada, whose 'asperities are there either omitted or watered down'. This made Mendoza's account generally very enthusiastic, presenting China as 'an enviable country, where justice was well administered, where the people were all prosperous and hard-working, peaceable and self-controlled.'[1]*

Mendoza was a Spanish Augustinian priest. In 1580 King Philip II of Spain, who had read de Rada's original account with great interest, decided to send an embassy to the Chinese Emperor and to invite Mendoza, who would take gifts such as pictures, clocks and watches, arms, and clothing. Mendoza's route to China passed through Mexico, where he had already lived for several years. For various reasons the embassy was aborted and Mendoza never got to China, but he did find much additional material about China in Mexico which he included in his book. Mendoza returned to Spain and went on to Rome, where he completed and published his great History.

The book was a great best-seller. By the end of the sixteenth century, it had been translated into all the main European languages and published in numerous editions. It was the basis of a new admiration for China in Europe, and of the great work which the Jesuits were to undertake. It can be considered the beginning of the first great age of Western sinology.

Indeed, it was so positive about China that the English printer felt called on to disavow any responsibility for offence given 'to the Christian reader' by the excessive zeal of the Spanish friars, arguing that these Catholic priests had a way of extolling their own actions, 'even to the setting forth of many untruths and incredible things'.[2]

The edition used is that translated by Robert Parke and printed in London in 1588. The title page gives the title of the book as The Historie of the Great and Mightie Kingdome of China and the Situation Thereof, Togither with the great riches, huge citties, politike gouernement, and rare inuentions in the same *and states that copies were 'Printed by I. Wolfe for Edward White, and are to be sold at the little North doore of Paules, at the signe of the Gun'. In the extracts below, I have replaced the original spelling with more contemporary spelling, but have otherwise left the language exactly as it was in the 1588 edition.*

The great travail and continual labour of the inhabitants of this country, is a great help unto the goodness and fertility thereof, and is so much that they do neither spare nor leave mountains nor valleys, neither rivers, but they do sow and plant all such things as they perceive that the place will yield, according unto the goodness thereof: as orchards with fruit, great fields of wheat, barley, rice, flax, and hemp, with many other things: all which travail unto them is very easy, remembering with what great liberty they do enjoy their goods, and the great and infinite number of people that there is, as well for handicrafts as for to till and cultivate the ground. In all this mighty country they do not suffer vagabonds nor idle people, but all such (over and above that they are grievously punished), they are holden for infamous: neither do they consent nor permit any of them that are naturally born there to go out of their countries into other strange countries; neither have they any wars at this present, which was the thing that in times past did consume much of their people. The king doth content himself only with his own kingdom (as one that is held the wisest in all the world). Beside all this, they are naturally inclined to eat and drink well, and to make much of themselves in apparel, and to have their houses well furnished with household stuff; and to the augmenting hereof, they do put themselves in great labour and travail, and are great dealers and traffickers: all which, with the fertility of the country above said, is the occasion that justify it might have the name to be the most fertilest in all the whole world.

Mendoza was impressed with the women of China, whom he describes as attractive and intelligent. He discusses the practice of bound feet which, in the marginal paragraph summaries so common in the sixteenth century, the printer has labelled 'an ill use and custom'.

They that be not married do differ from those that be married, in that they do curl their hair on their forehead, and wear higher hats. Their women do apparel themselves very curiously, much after the fashion of Spain: they use many jewels of gold and precious stones: their gowns have wide sleeves; that wherewith they do apparel themselves is of cloth of gold and silver and diverse sorts of silks, whereof they have great plenty, as aforesaid, and excellent good, and good cheap: and the poor folks do apparel themselves with velvet, unshorn velvet, and serge. They have very fair hair, and do comb it with great care and diligence, as do the women of Genoa, and do bind it about their head with a broad silk lace, set full of pearls and precious stones, and they say it doth become them very well: they do use to paint themselves, and in some place in excess.

Amongst them they account it for gentility and a gallant thing to have little feet, and therefore from their youth they so swaddle and bind them very straight, and do suffer it with patience: for that she who hath the least feet is accounted the gallantest dame. They say that the men hath induced them unto this custom, for to bind their feet so hard, that almost they do lose the form of them, and remain half lame, so that their going is very ill, and with great travail: which is the occasion that they go but little abroad, and few times do rise up from their work that they do; and was invented only for the same intent. This custom hath endured many years, and will endure many more, for that it is established for a law: and that woman which doth break it, and not use it with her children, shall be counted as evil, yea shall be punished for the same. They are very secret and honest, in such sort that you shall not see at any time a woman at her window nor at her doors: and if her husband do invite any person to dinner, she is never seen nor eateth not at the table, except the guest be a kinsman or a very friend: when they go abroad to visit their father, mother, or any other kinsfolk, they are carried in a little chair by four men, the which is made close, and with lattices round about made of gold wire and with silver, and curtains of silk; that although they do see them that be in the street, yet they cannot be seen. They have many servants waiting on them. So that it is a great marvel when that you shall meet a principal woman in the street, yea you will think that there are none in the city, their keeping in is such: the lameness of their feet is a great help thereunto. The women as well as the men be ingenious; they do use drawn works and carved works, excellent painters of flowers, birds, and beasts, as it is to be seen upon beds and boards that is brought from thence.

The following passage paints a rather mild picture of prisons. Although more horrific aspects are considered later, the system was probably no worse and no more unjust than the one which prevailed in Mendoza's own country at the time.

Even as the judges and ministers are severe and cruel in punishing, even so are they in putting them in prisons, the which are as terrible and as cruel, with the which they do keep in peace and justice this mighty kingdom: and as there is much people, so have they many prisons and very great. There are in every principal city throughout all these provinces thirteen prisons, enclosed and compassed about with high walls, and of so great largeness within, that besides the lodgings of the keeper and his officers, and for a garrison of soldiers that are there continually, there are fish ponds, gardens, and courts, whereas the prisoners do walk and recreate themselves all the day, such as are in for small matters. Likewise there are victualling houses and shops, whereas is sold all manner of such things as the prisoners do make for to sustain themselves; which if they did not use, their whole substance were not sufficient for their maintenance, the time is so long that they be there, although it be for a small matter: the occasion is for that the judges take deliberation in their sentences: and again, their cities are great and full of other matters. Likewise they are slow in the execution of any sentence. So that many times it doth fall out, that men being condemned to die, do remain so long in prison after their condemnation, that they die with pure age, or some other sickness or infirmity, or by the cruelty of the straight and asper prison. Of these thirteen prisons aforesaid, always four of them are occupied with prisoners condemned unto death, and in every one of them there is a captain over one hundred soldiers which are reparted, and doth keep watch and ward day and night: every one of these condemned prisoners hath a board tied about his neck that hangeth down unto his knees, a third of a yard broad; it is made white with a certain whiting, and written upon it the occasion wherefore he was condemned to die. The keeper of the prison hath a book, wherein is written all the names of them that are condemned, and the occasion wherefore: for to be accountable of them at all times when they shall be demanded of him by the judges or viceroys. They are shackled and manacled, and put in wards that do answer into the court, whereas the officers of the prison do make them to lie with the face downward upon a floor made of boards for the same purpose, and do draw over them iron chains, drawn through great iron rings that are placed betwixt prisoner and prisoner, wherewith they are so straight crushed that they cannot move nor turn them from one side to another: also they do lay on them a certain covering of timber, wherein remaineth no more space of hollowness than their bodies doth make: thus are they used that are condemned to death. This prison is so painful and grievous, that many do despair and kill themselves because they cannot suffer it. In the day time they do take them forth and take off their manacles, that they may work for to sustain themselves; all such as have nothing to maintain themselves, nor any other that will help them, them the king doth give a pittance of rice to sustain them. Likewise they do work what they may to better the same.

Mendoza shows himself aware of the examination system through which officials were chosen. His emphasis is on the grandeur of the ceremonies associated with it, but the following passage shows that he had some idea of its significance.

These visitors of whom we have spoken, the king and his council do send them to visit his provinces; and amongst the greatest things that are given them in charge, is the visitation of the colleges and schools which the king hath in all the principal cities, as is said; the which visitor hath a particular authority for to commence or graduate such students as have finished their course, and are of ability and sufficiency to perform the same. They do make them gentlemen, if they be capable of any charge of justice or government. . . .

At such time as the visitor hath concluded the visitation of his province, and hath punished the malefactors, and rewarded the good; in the metropolitan cities, he doth straightaway cause proclamation to be made that all students and scholars that do find themselves sufficient, and have a courage to be examined to take the degree of Loytia, the which, although amongst them is understood to be made a gentleman, yet amongst us is a doctor.

The day appointed being come, they are all presented before the visitor, who taketh all their names in a scroll, and appointeth another day for their examination. This day, for honour of the feast, the visitor doth invite all the learned Loytias that are in the city, who jointly with him do make the examination with great rigour, always putting forwards and preferring those that are skilful in the laws of the country, by which they do govern all other faculties whatsoever, and that they be therewithal good, and virtuous. And all those that they do find with these properties, they do write their names in another scroll, and do appoint the day of commencement, the which is done with great ceremonies and much people, in whose presence the visitor, in the name of the king, doth give unto them the ensigns of degree and dignity to be a Loytia; that is, a waist or girdle bossed with gold or silver, and a hat with certain things on it, as shall be shown you in the chapter following; which is a sign and token that doth make the difference from the vulgar people, without the which none can show himself in public.

PART III

THE EARLY JESUITS

The policy of the Jesuits towards China was broad-minded. In essence, they were happy to adopt Chinese culture as far as they could, even in matters of religious ceremonies, providing no conflict arose with the doctrines of the Catholic Church. This policy got them into trouble with other religious orders, such as the Dominicans and Franciscans, as well as with Rome. In 1715, Pope Clement XI condemned the policy of the Jesuits, coming down firmly on the side of the Jesuits' enemies in the so-called 'rites controversy'. In 1742, Pope Benedict XIV reaffirmed the ban on Jesuit policy and forbade further debate over the matter. Jesuit withdrawal from China accelerated after this time, and the final death knell for this phase of their activity in China was rung in 1774, when news reached Beijing of papal suppression of the Jesuits the preceding year.

In the meantime, however, the Jesuits had sent home a deluge of information and insights about China, forming collectively by far the most voluminous and intelligent material on China written in the West up to that time. There were several major series of letters, journals, and other documents, the most important being *Lettres édifiantes et curieuses*, published from 1703 to 1776, of which about one-third concerned China.

5

CRUEL CONSIDERATIONS

MATTEO RICCI

TRANSLATED BY FATHER LOUIS GALLAGHER

Father Matteo Ricci SJ (1552–1610), the most famous of the pre-nineteenth-century Catholic missionaries in China, lived there for the last thirty-odd years of his life. His method of Christianizing China was to start at the top of society, with the influential and prestigious bureaucracy, and to immerse himself in Chinese culture rather than expecting the Chinese to take on European customs. Ricci left a diary, in Italian, of his experiences. It mostly records of the work of his mission, but contains some commentary on the China he found around him. However, he did not intend it to be published and it did not see the light of day in his own time. After his death it was brought back to Rome and translated into Latin by Father Nicola Trigault, SJ, who had it published in Rome in 1615. The 1942 edition from which the extracts below are taken is the first in English.

Ricci worked in China in the late years of the Ming dynasty (1368–1644). His impressions are much less laudatory than those of the Jesuits in the 150 years following his death. Yet he also has positive things to say about China and the Chinese, and praises their filial piety and love of peace. Although the Ming has a reasonably good reputation among historians as the last of the fully Chinese dynasties to rule China, its last decades were beset with problems and it is striking that Ricci's impressions of China are not more negative still. Certainly, he and his Jesuit followers did better from the Chinese legal system than the average Chinese, even though he complains of persecutions against Christians. The following extracts recount the darker side of the Chinese life he observed.

We shall add here a few shocking practices which the Chinese look upon with indifference and which, God forbid, they even seem to consider as quite morally correct, and from these one can readily conclude to others of the same category. This people is really to be pitied rather than censured, and the deeper one finds them involved in the darkness of ignorance, the more earnest one should be in praying for their salvation.

Many of them, not being able to forgo the company of women, sell themselves to wealthy patrons, so as to find a wife among his women servants, and in so doing, subject their children to perpetual slavery. Others buy a wife when they can save money enough to do so, and when their family becomes too numerous to be supported, they sell their children into slavery for about the same price that one would pay for a pig or a cheap little donkey—about one crown or maybe one and a half. Sometimes this is done when there is really no necessity, and children are separated from their parents forever, becoming slaves to the purchaser, to be used for whatever purpose he pleases. The result of this practice is that the whole country is virtually filled with slaves; not such as are captured in war or brought in from abroad, but slaves born in the country and even in the same city or village in which they live. Many of them are also taken out of the country as slaves by the Portuguese and the Spaniards. . . .

A far more serious evil here is the practice in some provinces of disposing of female infants by drowning them. The reason assigned for this is that their parents despair of being able to support them. At times this is also done by people who are not abjectly poor, for fear the time might come when they would not be able to care for these children and they would be forced to sell them to unknown or to cruel slave masters. Thus they become cruel in an effort to be considerate. This barbarism is probably rendered less atrocious by their belief in metempsychosis, or the transmigration of souls. Believing that souls are transferred from one body that ceases to exist into another that begins to exist, they cover up their frightful cruelty with a pretext of piety, thinking that they are doing the child a benefit by murdering it. According to their way of thinking, they are releasing the child from the poverty of the family into which it was born, so that it may be reborn into a family of better means. So it happens that this slaughter of the

The Procession of a Chinese Wedding, eighteenth century. Source: J. B. Du Halde, *The General History of China.*

innocents is carried on not in secret but in the open with general public knowledge. . . .

Yet another barbarity common in the northern provinces is that of castrating a great number of male children, so they may act as servants or as slaves to the King. This condition is demanded for service in the royal palace, so much so, indeed, that the King will have no others nor will he consult with or even speak to any other. Almost the whole administration of the entire kingdom is in the hands of this class of semi-men, who number nearly ten thousand in the service of the royal palace alone. They are a meager-looking class, uneducated and brought up in perpetual slavery, a dull and stolid lot, as incapable of understanding an important order as they are inefficient in carrying it out.

The penal laws of the country do not seem to be too severe, but it seems that as many are illegally put to death by the magistrates as are legally executed. This is brought about by a fixed and ancient custom of the country permitting a magistrate, without any legal process or judgment, to subject a person to flogging when it might please him to do so. This punishment is administered in public. The victim, lying prone, face down to the ground, is beaten on the bare legs and buttocks with a tough reed, split down the middle, about an inch thick, four inches wide, and about a yard long. The executioners swing this flail with both hands and strike unmercifully. The regular number of blows is ten, with thirty as a limit, but the first blow usually breaks the skin and the flesh flies about in the subsequent beating, with the result that the victim frequently dies from the flogging. At times the accused will buy off his life by paying a high price to the magistrate, contrary to all law and justice.

So great is the lust for domination on the part of the magistrates that scarcely anyone can be said to possess his belongings in security, and every one lives in continual fear of being deprived of what he has, by a false accusation. Just as this people is grossly subject to superstition, so, too, they have very little regard for the truth, acting always with great circumspection, and very cautious about trusting anyone. Subject to this same fear, the kings of modern times abandoned the custom of going out in public.

A MILD AND AFFABLE PEOPLE

J. B. DU HALDE

TRANSLATED BY R. BROOKES

The French Jesuit J. B. Du Halde (1674–1743) was the editor of Volumes IX to XXVI of the Lettres édifiantes et curieuses *(1709–43). They were the main source for his magnum opus* The General History of China, *itself the most important and comprehensive single product of Jesuit scholarship on China. Published in French in 1736, this major landmark in the history of sinology was immediately translated into English and other European languages. Among those who used it as a source were Montesquieu, Rousseau, Voltaire, Hume, and Goldsmith.*

Du Halde never visited China. However, according to the first page of the preface in Volume 1, 'fearing lest any error might possibly have escaped him, he had thoughts of sending the work into China to be reviewed by some of the Jesuits residing there; when the arrival of P. Contancin, on whom he had chiefly cast his eyes, rendered it unnecessary'. Contancin, so the preface continues, had lived in China for thirty-two years, ten of them in Beijing as the Superior of the Jesuit house there. He stayed in Paris for a year, and so had time 'to alter, add, or retrench whatever he thought necessary for the perfection of the design'.

Du Halde was positive, even laudatory about China, frequently making comparisons with Europe to show better conditions in China. He refused to accept the view of an atheistic Chinese culture and even selected material through which he could refute such an opinion. Given that the papacy had already come down against the Jesuits in the rites controversy, this was a daring position to adopt.

Of the Genius and Character of the Chinese

The Chinese in general are mild, tractable, and humane; there is a great deal of affability in their air and manner, and nothing harsh, rough, or passionate: this moderation is remarkable among the vulgar themselves: 'I was one day (says Pere de Fontaney) in a narrow long lane, where there happened in a short time a great stop of the carriages; I expected they would have fallen into a passion, used opprobrious language, and perhaps have come to blows, as is very common in Europe; but I was much surprised to see that they saluted each other, spoke mildly, as if they had been old acquaintances, and lent their mutual assistance to pass each other.'

They shew a great deal of deference and respect for their old men, of which the Emperor himself sets an example to his people: an inferior Mandarin of the Tribunal of the Mathematicks, about a hundred years old, came to court the first day of the Chinese Year to salute the late Emperor Cang hi [Kangxi]; this Prince, who designed to see no body that day, gave orders however that he should be admitted; as the good old man was but indifferently habited, every one was forward to supply him on that occasion; they conducted him into the Emperor's apartment, who was sitting in an alcove after the Tartarian manner; he rose up and went to meet him, and received him with great sign of affection; the Mandarin fell upon his knees, but the Emperor immediately raised him up, and graciously taking both his hands, *'Venerable Old Man'*, said he, *'I will admit you henceforth into my presence as often as you shall come to salute me; but I acquaint you, once for all, that I dispense with all sorts of ceremony; as for me, I will rise up to meet you, but it is not to your person that I do this honour, it is to your age; and to give you substantial marks of my affection, I now appoint you to be Chief President of the Tribunal of the Mathematicks.'* Thus the old man attained the height of happiness, having never in his life tasted so sincere a joy.

When you have to do with a Chinese you must take care of being too hasty or warm; the genius of the country requires that we should master our passions, and act with a great deal of calmness; the Chinese would not hear patiently in a month what a Frenchman can speak in an hour; one must suffer, without taking fire, this phlegm that seems more natural to them than any other nation; it is not because they want fire or vivacity, but they learn

This picture has become famous as a positive eighteenth-century image of Confucius, the Chinese philosopher noted for his wisdom and grasp of political ethics. Source: J. B. Du Halde, *The General History of China.*

betimes to become masters of themselves, and value themselves in being more polite and more civilized than other nations. . . .

If the Chinese are mild and peaceable in conversation, and when they are not provoked, they are exceeding violent and revengeful when they are offended; the following is an instance: It was perceived in a maritime province that a Mandarin had misapplied, for his own advantage, a great part of the rice sent thither by the Emperor in a time of dearth to be distributed to every family in the country; the people accused him before a Superior Tribunal, and proved that out of the four hundred load of rice that he had received he had dispensed but ninety, upon which the Mandarin was immediately deprived of his office.

. . . As for the women they are commonly middle-sized, their noses short, their eyes little, their mouth well made, their lips rosy, their hair black, their ears long, and their complexion florid; there is a great deal of vivacity in their countenance, and their features are very regular.

It is said that they rub their faces every morning with a kind of paint that sets off the whiteness of their complexion, and gives them a colour, but soon spoils their skin and makes it full of wrinkles.

31

Among the charms of the sex the smallness of their feet is not the least; when a female infant comes into the world, the nurses are very careful to bind their Feet very close for fear they should grow too large: the Chinese ladies are subject all their lives to this constraint, which they were accustomed to in their infancy, and their gait is slow, unsteady, and disagreeable to foreigners: yet such is the force of custom, that they not only undergo this inconvenience readily, but they increase it, and endeavour to make their feet as little as possible, thinking it an extraordinary charm, and always affecting to shew them as they walk.

One cannot certainly say what is the reason of such an odd custom, for the Chinese themselves do not pretend to be certain, looking upon that story to be fabulous, which attributes the invention to the ancient Chinese, who, to oblige their wives to keep at home, are said to have brought little feet into fashion. The far greater number think it to be a politick design, in order to keep the women in a constant dependance: it is very certain that they seldom stir out of their apartment, which is in the most inward part of the house, having no communication with any but the women-servants.

However they have, generally speaking, the common vanity of the sex, and tho' they are not to be seen but by their domesticks, they spend several hours every morning in dressing and adorning themselves. Their head-dress consists in several curls interspersed with little tufts of gold and silver flowers. . . .

That which sets off the natural charms of the Chinese ladies, is the uncommon modesty which appears in their looks and their dress; their gowns are very long, and cover them from head to foot in such a manner that nothing appears but their face. Their hands are always concealed under wide long sleeves, that would almost drag on the Ground if they were not careful to lift them up. The colour of their garments is various, either red, blue, or green, according to their fancy; none but ladies advanced in years wear violet or black.

As for what is here called the fashion, it has nothing at all in it like what we call so in Europe, where the manner of dress is subject to many changes. It is not so in China, which is a sign of good order, and the uniformity of the government, even in the most trifling matters; for which reason the fashion of dress has been always the same from the infancy of the empire to the conquest of it by the Tartars [Manchus], who without changing the form of the ancient Chinese Government have only obliged them to dress in their manner.

PART IV

ENLIGHTENMENT AND DECEIT

The thinkers of the age of the Enlightenment, which reached its height in the eighteenth century, placed greater emphasis on reason as an instrument for arriving at truth than their predecessors of the Renaissance, let alone of the Middle Ages. The Enlightenment profoundly influenced philosophy and the arts, and saw the beginnings of the modern social sciences. There was intense debate over government, society, and economic matters. On the whole, eighteenth-century thinkers were well disposed towards China, appreciating its secular approach to government and admiring its prosperity. However, there was also a strong trend opposite to the prevailing one.

SPLENDID SECULAR GOVERNANCE

VOLTAIRE

The most important member of what we might term 'the pro-China lobby' was Voltaire (1694–1778). He was undoubtedly the most influential of the French philosophers and historians of his day and his role in creating a positive image of China in the eighteenth century was of the utmost significance.

Among Voltaire's prodigious output were several dramas, including L'orphélin de la Chine (Orphan of China), first produced in 1755. This was based on the Chinese drama Zhaoshi gu'er (Orphan of the Zhao Family), part of which had been translated into French and published in 1736 in the English translation in Volume 3 of Du Halde's great work.

What impressed Voltaire most of all was the secular nature of Confucianism, and the fact that the clergy were not allowed to take part in government. This point comes through strongly in the following extract, from a work which Voltaire published in 1766 in London and which closely reflects his attitudes towards life and reality.

Never was the religion of the emperors and the tribunals dishonored with impostures; never was it troubled with quarrels between the priests and the empire; never was it burdened with absurd innovations, which are supported one against the other by arguments as absurd as themselves, the rage of which has at length placed the poignard in the hands of fanatics led on by the factious. Here the Chinese are particularly superior to all the nations of the universe.

Their Confucius framed neither new opinions nor new rites. He neither pretended to be an inspired man, nor a prophet. He was a magistrate, who taught the ancient laws. We sometimes say, very improperly, 'the religion of Confucius'; he had no other than that of all the emperors and all the tribunals; no other than that of the first sages; he recommends nothing but virtue, preaches no mysteries; he says, in his first book, that in order to learn to govern, we should pass our whole life in correcting ourselves; in the second, he proves that God has himself graven virtue in the heart of man; he says that man is not born wicked, and that he becomes so by his own fault; the third is a collection of pure maxims, where we can meet with nothing that is mean, nor any ridiculous allegories. He had five thousand disciples, he might have put himself at the head of a powerful party; but he rather chose to instruct men, than to govern them. . . .

The magistrates conceived that the people might have different religions from that of the state, as they live upon grosser aliment; they suffered the bonzes, and continued them. In almost every other country, those who carried on the trade of bonzes, had the principal authority.

The following extract is from a substantial entry on China in Voltaire's multi-volume Dictionnaire philosophique. *While it contrasts the West favourably with China in some respects, the entry praises China with the assertion that its civilization compares very favourably indeed with those of other nations, in particular Europe.*

Were it worth our while, we might here compare the great wall of China with the monuments of other nations, which have never even approached it; and remark that, in comparison with this extensive work, the pyramids of Egypt are only puerile and useless masses. We might dwell on the thirty-two eclipses calculated in the ancient chronology of China, twenty-eight of which have been verified by the mathematicians of Europe. We might show that the respect entertained by the Chinese for their ancestors is an evidence that such ancestors have existed; and repeat the observation, so often made, that this reverential respect has in no small degree impeded, among this people, the progress of natural philosophy, geometry, and astronomy.

It is sufficiently known that they are, at the present day, what we all were three hundred years ago, very ignorant reasoners. The most learned Chinese is like one of the learned of Europe in the fifteenth century, in possession of his Aristotle. But it is possible to be a very bad natural philosopher, and at the same time an excellent moralist. It is, in fact, in morality, in political economy, in agriculture, in the necessary arts of life, that the Chinese have made such advances towards perfection. All the rest they have been taught by us: in these we might well submit to become their disciples. . . .

Of the Pretended Atheism of China

The charge of Atheism, alleged by our theologians of the west, against the Chinese government at the other end of the world, has been frequently examined,[1] and is, it must be admitted, the meanest excess of our follies and pedantic inconsistencies. It was sometimes pretended, in one of our learned faculties, that the Chinese tribunals or parliaments, were idolatrous; sometimes that they acknowledged no divinity whatever: and these reasoners occasionally pushed their logic so far as to maintain that the Chinese were, at the same time, atheists and idolaters.

In the month of October, 1700 the Sorbonne declared every proposition, which maintained that the emperor and the Colaos [mandarins] believed in God, to be heretical. Bulky volumes were composed in order to demonstrate, conformably to the system of theological demonstration, that the Chinese adored nothing but the material heaven.

> Nil praeter nubes et coeli numen adorant.
> They worship clouds and firmament alone.

But if they did adore the material heaven, that was their God. They resembled the Persians, who are said to have adored the sun: they resembled the ancient Arabians, who adored the stars. They were neither worshippers of idols nor atheists. . . .

The celebrated Wolfe,[2] professor of mathematics in the University of Halle,[3] delivered once an excellent discourse in praise of the Chinese philosophy. He praised that ancient species of the human race, differing, as it does, in respect to the beard, the eyes, the nose, the ears, and even the reasoning powers themselves; he praised the Chinese, I say, for their adoration of a supreme God, and their love of virtue. He did that justice to the emperors of China, to the tribunals, and to the literati. The justice done to the bonzes was of a different kind.

It is necessary to observe that this professor Wolfe had attracted around him a thousand pupils of all nations. In the same university there was also a professor of theology, who attracted no one. This man, maddened at the thought of freezing to death in his own deserted hall, formed the design, which undoubtedly was only right and reasonable, of destroying the mathematical professor. He scrupled not, according to the practice of persons like himself, to accuse him of not believing in God.

Some European writers, who had never been in China, had pretended that the government of Pekin was atheistical. Wolfe had praised the philosophers of Pekin; therefore Wolfe was an atheist.[4]

Voltaire goes on to explain that the excellent Professor Wolf was offered the choice of leaving Hall at a day's notice or be hanged. He chose the former alternative. Voltaire observes drily that 'this case should convince sovereigns that they ought not to be over ready to listen to calumny, and sacrifice a great man to the madness of a fool.' The number of students whom Professor Wolf attracted, apparently in large part for his sensible views on China, gives a good idea of where Voltaire believed intelligent and educated opinion to lie on this matter.

One of Voltaire's main historical works, Essai sur les moeurs et l'esprit des nations, *can probably claim to be the first in any language to attempt to cover the history of the whole world. Although Europe gets fuller coverage than any other continent, Voltaire included chapters on India, the Muslim world, and Africa. And of course there are several chapters on China.*

In the following extract, Voltaire comments on the reign and person of the Yongzheng Emperor (r. 1723–35). As the reader can see, the Chinese emperor scores high marks from Voltaire, despite his policies of hostility towards the Christian missionaries. Apparently the comments are intended to apply to Chinese governance generally. As extremely recent history at the time Voltaire was writing, this section comes near the end of his remarkable historical work. It is notable that he quotes from the Lettres édifiantes et curieuses *of the Jesuits.*

The successor of Cam-hi [Kangxi] prohibited the practice of the Christian religion, but permitted Islam and the different kinds of bonzes. But this same court, in the belief that mathematics was as necessary as the new religion was dangerous, kept the mathematicians, imposing silence on the remainder and expelling the missionaries. This emperor, named Yong-ching [Yongzheng], said to them the following, which they have had the good faith to report in their letters entitled *curious and edifying*.

What would you say if I sent a group of bonzes and lamas into your country? How would you receive them? You knew how to deceive my father, but don't hope to deceive me as well. You want the Chinese to embrace your law. Your cult tolerates no other, I know that. In that case what would we become? The subjects of your princes. The disciples you make know only you, and in a time of trouble they would listen to no voice other than yours. I know that at present there is nothing to fear; but when the ships come in their thousands, there could be political disorder.

The same Jesuits who have taken account of these words admit with all others that this emperor was one of the wisest and most generous princes who has ever reigned. He was always concerned with alleviating the plight of the poor and putting them to work. He observed the law carefully, he curbed the ambitions and deceits of the bonzes, maintaining peace and prosperity, encouraging all useful skills and arts, and above all the cultivation of the land. From his time public buildings, large-scale highways, canals joining all the rivers of this great empire, were maintained with a splendour and thrift which has no equal other than among the ancient Romans.

8
ENLIGHTENED DESPOTISM

FRANÇOIS QUESNAY

TRANSLATED BY COLIN MACKERRAS

Almost exactly contemporary with Voltaire was François Quesnay (1694–1774), who worked as a physician at the court of King Louis XV at Versailles. Quesnay became interested in economics and in his sixties began publishing on that subject. He was the main founder and leader of a group known as the physiocrats.

The physiocrats are regarded as the first scientific school of economics. Their main idea was that economics should follow the rule of nature. The implication was that governments should not interfere in the economy, which should be allowed to follow the moral laws of nature. They also believed land to be the source of all wealth.

Quesnay admired China enormously. In particular, China was a kind of model for his ideas on the economic importance of agriculture. In the following passage he develops his notions concerning the prosperity and fairness of Chinese agriculture.

The small people of China live almost entirely on grain, herbs, or vegetables, and in no place in the world are kitchen gardens commoner or better cultivated. There is no uncultivated land near the towns, no trees, hedges or ditches, for fear that even the smallest plot of land would remain useless.

In the southern provinces, the land never remains fallow, even the hills and mountains are cultivated from foot to summit. There is nothing more admirable than a long row of hills, surrounded and as if crowned by a hundred terraces, which contract in size as one nears the top. With surprise one can see here mountains which elsewhere would scarcely produce brambles or thickets, become a laughing image of fertility.

Land generally yields three harvests a year, the first rice, the second what has been sown before the rice is harvested, and the third broadbeans or some other grains. The Chinese spare no pains to collect all sorts of refuse proper to fertilizing their land, which has the added advantage of keeping their towns clean. All grains we know in Europe, such as wheat, rice, oats, millet, peas, broadbeans, grow also in China.

The custom is for the owner of the land to take half the crops and that he pay the taxes. The other half stays with the labourer for his expenses and his work. In that country the lands are not encumbered with ecclesiastical tithes. The labourer's portion is about in the same proportion as the farmer's in this country, in the provinces where the lands are well cultivated.

In China farm labourers are regarded as higher in status than merchants or artisans. . . . Agriculture has always been venerated and those who carry it out have always merited the particular attention of the emperors.

Quesnay had strong views on the subject of despotisms. He divided them into the good and the bad; China was despotic, but a good country nevertheless.

We can conclude that the Chinese government is a despotism, because the sovereign of this empire unites all supreme authority in himself alone. *Despot* means master or lord: so this title can extend to sovereigns who exercise absolute power ruled by laws, and to sovereigns who have usurped arbitrary power, which they exercise for better or worse over nations the governments of which are not assured by basic laws. Thus there are legitimate despots, and arbitrary and illegitimate despots. . . .

The emperor of China is a despot. But in what sense can we give him this name? It seems to me that, generally speaking, we in Europe have very unfavourable views on this empire's government. But on the contrary I have come to realize from accounts about China that its constitution is based on wise and irrevocable laws, which the emperor enforces and which he himself observes exactly.

9
A MOST UNSCRUPULOUS PEOPLE

MONTESQUIEU

TRANSLATED BY ANNE M. COHLER,

BASIA CAROLYN MILLER, AND SAMUEL HAROLD STONE

Among the thinkers of the French Enlightenment, the one most notable for his hostility to China was Charles-Louis de Secondat, Baron de La Brède et de Montesquieu (1689–1755), usually known simply by the last of these names. Montesquieu was a political philosopher whose main work, L'esprit des lois *(The Spirit of the Laws), first appeared in 1748 and made a strong contribution to the history of political theory.*

This work divided states into three kinds. The most benign was the republic, then the monarchy, and the most oppressive was despotism. Unusually, Montesquieu's ideas attributed a moral principle to each of these. He believed the republic to be based on virtue, the monarchy on honour, and despotism on fear. In contrast to Quesnay, he thus saw despotism as evil almost by its nature. He agreed with Quesnay in categorizing China as a despotism, but differed sharply by condemning it for that reason.

Our missionaries speak of the vast empire of China as of an admirable government, in whose principle intermingle fear, honour, and virtue. I would therefore have made an empty distinction in establishing the principles of the three governments.

I do not know how one can speak of honour among peoples who can be made to do nothing without beatings.

Moreover, our men of commerce, far from giving us an idea of the same kind of virtue of which our missionaries speak, can rather be consulted about the banditry of the mandarins. I also call to witness the great man, Lord Anson.[1]. . .

The climate of China is such that it prodigiously favours the reproduction of mankind. Women there have such great fertility that nothing like it is seen elsewhere on earth. The cruellest tyranny cannot check the progress of propagation. The prince cannot say with the Pharaoh, *Let us oppress them wisely.* He would be reduced, rather, to formulating Nero's wish that mankind should have only one head. Despite tyranny, China, because of its climate, will always populate itself and will triumph over tyranny.

China, like all countries where rice is grown, is subject to frequent famines. When the people are starving, they scatter to seek something to eat. Everywhere bands of three, four, or five robbers form: most are immediately wiped out; others grow and are also wiped out. But, in such a great number of distant provinces, a group may meet with success. It maintains itself, grows stronger, forms itself into an army, goes straight to the capital, and its leader comes to the throne.

The nature of the thing is such that bad government there is immediately punished. Disorder is born suddenly when this prodigious number of people lacks subsistence. What makes it so hard to recover from abuses in other countries is that the effects are not felt; the prince is not alerted as promptly and strikingly as in China.

He will not feel, as our princes do, that if he governs badly, he will be less happy in the next life, less powerful, and less rich in this one; he will know that, if his government is not good, he will lose his empire and his life.

As the Chinese people become ever more numerous despite exposing their children, they must work tirelessly to make the lands produce enough to feed themselves; this demands great attention on the part of the government. It is in its interest for everyone at every moment to be able to work without fear of being frustrated for his pains. This should be less a civil government than a domestic government.

This is what has produced the rules that are so much discussed. Some have wanted to have laws reign along with despotism, but whatever is joined to despotism no longer has force. This despotism, beset by its misfortunes, has wanted in vain to curb itself; it arms itself with its chains and becomes yet more terrible.

Therefore, China is a despotic state whose principle is fear. In the first dynasties, when the empire was not so extensive, perhaps the government deviated a little from that spirit, but that is not so today.

Another of Montesquieu's most famous notions was that climate influences the political, intellectual, and social nature of a people. Law can, and should, act against the bad side of this nature to bring about general political and social improvement. But in the case of China the climate has made the state despotic and the people dishonest, while the laws, though they may tend to make the people hard-working, nevertheless also exacerbate the deceit of the people and the oppression which is their lot.

It is strange that the Chinese, whose life is entirely directed by rites, are nevertheless the most unscrupulous people on earth. This appears chiefly in commerce, which has never been able to inspire in them the good faith natural to it. The buyer should carry his own scale as each merchant has three of them, a heavy one for buying, a light one for selling, and an accurate one for those who are on their guard. I believe I can explain this contradiction.

Chinese legislators have had two objects: they have wanted the people to be both submissive and tranquil, and hardworking and industrious. Because of the nature of the climate and the terrain, their life is precarious; one secures one's life there only by dint of industry and work.

When everyone obeys and everyone works, the state is in a fortunate situation. Necessity and perhaps the nature of the climate have given all the Chinese an unthinkable avidity for gain, and the laws have not dreamed of checking it. Everything has been prohibited if it is a question of acquisition by violence; everything has been permitted if it is a matter of obtaining by artifice or by industry. Therefore, let us not compare the morality of China with that of Europe. Everyone in China has had to be attentive to what was useful to him; if the rascal has watched over his interests, he who is duped has had to think of his own. In Lacedaemonia, stealing was permitted; in China, deceit is permitted.

PART V

ECONOMIC IMPERATIVES

The glorified image of Chinese government as a benign despotism, which men like Du Halde, Voltaire, and Quesnay had endorsed, tended to sour as the eighteenth century wore on. An important factor in this change was the extremely negative view put forward in the account of Baron George Anson's visit to Guangdong province in the summer of 1743. Baron Anson (1697–1762) led a voyage around the world from 1740 to 1744, most of it in one ship, the *Centurion*, which became the first British warship ever to enter Chinese waters.

10

JESUITICAL FICTIONS

RICHARD WALTER AND BENJAMIN ROBINS

*The account of Anson's voyage, written by Richard Walter (1716–1785)
and Benjamin Robins (1707–51) from papers and materials by Anson
himself, was first published in May 1748 and attracted over 1,800 advance
subscribers, including eminent people. By the end of the year, the Anson
account had gone through four more editions. It appealed to the British as
a story of adventure at sea and also for its advocacy of the expansion of
British power and commerce in the Pacific. As we saw in Part IV,
Montesquieu knew and admired the work of Lord Anson, and his Spirit of
the Laws was published in the same year.*

  *Walter and Robins frequently scoff at the prevailing view of China in
works such as those by Voltaire and the Jesuits. They paint the Chinese as
interested only in money and as mendacious thieves. The government of
China comes over not as the ideal painted by the Jesuits but as corrupt and
oppressive. The following extract, from near the end of the account of the
voyage, represents Anson's summation of China and the Chinese.*

That the Chinese are a very ingenious and industrious people
is sufficiently evinced from the great number of curious
manufactures which are established amongst them, and
which are eagerly sought for by the most distant nations; but
though skill in the handicraft arts seems to be the most important
qualification of this people, yet their talents therein are but of a
second rate kind; for they are much outdone by the Japanese in
those manufactures, which are common to both countries; and
they are in numerous instances incapable of rivalling the mechanic
dexterity of the Europeans. Indeed, their principal excellency
seems to be imitation; and they accordingly labour under the
poverty of genius, which constantly attends all servile imitators. . . .
In short, there is a stiffness and minuteness in most of the Chinese

productions, which are extremely displeasing. And it may perhaps be asserted with great truth, that these defects in their arts are entirely owing to the peculiar turn of the people, amongst whom nothing great or spirited is to be met with. . . .

But we are told by some of the missionaries that though the skill of the Chinese in science is indeed much inferior to that of the Europeans, yet the morality and justice taught and practised by them are most exemplary. And from the description given by some of these good fathers, one should be induced to believe that the whole Empire was a well-governed affectionate family, where the only contests were, who should exert the most humanity and beneficence: But our preceding relation of the behaviour of the magistrates, merchants, and tradesmen at Canton sufficiently refutes these Jesuitical fictions. And as to their theories of morality, if we may judge from the specimens exhibited in the works of the missionaries, we shall find them solely employed in recommending ridiculous attachments to certain immaterial points, instead of discussing the proper criterion of human actions, and regulating the general conduct of mankind to one another, on reasonable and equitable principles. Indeed, the only pretension of the Chinese to a more refined morality than their neighbours is founded not on their integrity or beneficence, but solely on the affected evenness of their demeanor, and their constant attention to suppress all symptoms of passion and violence. But it must be considered, that hypocrisy and fraud are often not less mischievous to the general interests of mankind than impetuosity and vehemence of temper: Since these, though usually liable to the imputation of imprudence, do not exclude sincerity, benevolence, resolution, nor many other laudable qualities. And perhaps, if this matter was examined to the bottom, it would appear that the calm and patient turn of the Chinese, on which they so much value themselves, and which distinguishes the Nation from all others, is in reality the source of the most exceptionable part of their character; for it has been often observed by those who have attended to the nature of mankind that it is difficult to curb the more robust and violent passions without augmenting, at the same time, the force of the selfish ones: So that the timidity, dissimulation, and dishonesty of the Chinese, may, in some sort, be owing to the composure, and external decency, so universally prevailing in that Empire.

Thus much for the general disposition of the people: But I cannot dismiss this subject without adding a few words about the Chinese Government, that too having been the subject of boundless panegyric. And on this head I must observe that the favourable accounts often given of their prudent regulations for the administration of their domestic affairs are sufficiently confuted by their transactions with Mr Anson: For we have seen that their Magistrates are corrupt, their people thievish, and their tribunals crafty and venal. Nor is the constitution of the Empire or the general orders of the State less liable to exception: Since that form of Government, which does not in the first place provide for the security of the public against the enterprises of foreign powers, is certainly a most defective institution: And yet this populous, this rich and extensive country, so pompously celebrated for its refined wisdom and policy, was conquered about an age since by a handful of Tartars; and even now, by the cowardice of the inhabitants, and the want of proper military regulations, it continues exposed not only to the attempts of any potent state, but to the ravages of every petty invader.

11
HORRID OFFICES

ADAM SMITH

The Scot Adam Smith (1723–90) enjoys an extremely high reputation for his enormous and innovative contribution to the history of ideas on economics and social evolution. His Wealth of Nations, *first published in 1776, is his most famous work and the classic of laissez-faire economics. In it he argues, among a large range of other historical, social, and economic ideas, that free competition is the key to economic and social advance.*

Smith's view of China was positive in some ways, but not in others. He admired its fertility and size, and did not see it as declining. On the other hand, he was fiercely condemnatory of the fact that it never seemed to change, and that ordinary people were prepared to put up with poverty without trying to better their condition.

China has been long one of the richest, that is, one of the most fertile, best cultivated, most industrious, and most populous countries in the world. It seems, however, to have been long stationary. Marco Polo, who visited it more than five hundred years ago, describes its cultivation, industry, and populousness, almost in the same terms in which they are described by travellers in the present times. It had, perhaps even long before his time, acquired that full complement of riches which the nature of its laws and institutions permits it to acquire. The account of all travellers, inconsistent in many other respects, agree in the low wages of labour, and in the difficulty which a labourer finds in bringing up a family in China. If by digging the ground a whole day he can get what will purchase a small quantity of rice in the evening, he is contented. The condition of artificers is, if possible, still worse. Instead of waiting indolently in their work-houses for the calls of their customers, as in Europe, they are continually running about the streets with the tools of their respective trades, offering their services, and, as it were, begging employment. The poverty of the lower ranks of people in China far surpasses that of the most beggarly nations in Europe. In the neighbourhood of Canton, many hundred, it is commonly said, many thousand families have no habitation on the land, but live constantly in little fishing-boats upon the rivers and canals. The subsistence which they find there is so scanty, that they are eager to fish up the nastiest garbage thrown overboard from any European ship. Any carrion, the carcase of a dead dog or cat, for example, though half putrid and stinking, is as welcome to them as the most wholesome food to the people of other countries. Marriage is encouraged in China, not by the profitableness of children, but by the liberty of destroying them. In all great towns, several are every night exposed in the street, or drowned like puppies in the water. The performance of this horrid office is even said to be the avowed business by which some people earn their subsistence.

China, however, though it may perhaps stand still, does not seem to go backwards. Its town are nowhere deserted by their inhabitants. The lands which had once been cultivated, are nowhere neglected.

Smith admired much about China's economy, its extensive internal trade and communications, and its variety of manufactures. On the other hand, his ideas on free competition made him extremely suspicious of China's lack of international trade, which he believed had held the country back in a range of ways, and would likely continue to do so.

The policy of China favours agriculture more than all other employments. In China, the condition of a labourer is said to be as much superior to that of an artificer, as in most parts of Europe that of an artificer is to that of a labourer. In China, the great ambition of every man is to get possession of a little bit of land, either in property or in lease; and leases are there said to be granted upon very moderate terms, and to be sufficiently secured to the lessees. The Chinese have little respect for foreign trade. Your beggarly commerce! was the language in which the mandarins of Pekin used to talk to Mr De Lange, the Russian envoy, concerning it. Except with Japan, the Chinese carry on themselves, and in their own bottoms, little or no foreign trade; and it is only into one or two ports of their kingdom that they even admit the ships of foreign nations. Foreign trade, therefore, is, in China, every way confined within a much narrower circle than that to which it would naturally extend itself if more freedom were allowed to it, either in their own ships or in those of foreign nations.

Manufactures, as in a small bulk they frequently contain a great value, and can upon that account be transported at less expense from one country to another than more parts of rude produce, are, in almost all countries, the principal support of foreign trade. In countries, besides, less extensive and less favourably circumstanced for inferior commerce than China, they generally require the support of foreign trade. Without an extensive foreign market, they could not well flourish, either in countries so moderately extensive as to afford but a narrow home market, or in countries where the communication between one province and another was so difficult as to render it impossible for the goods of any particular place to enjoy the whole of that home market which the country could afford. The perfection of manufacturing industry, it must be remembered, depends altogether upon the division of labour; and the degree to which the division of labour can be introduced into any manufacture is necessarily regulated, it has already been shown, by the extent of the market. But the great extent of the empire of China, the vast multitude of its inhabitants, the variety of climate, and consequently of productions in its different provinces, and the easy communication by means of water-carriage between the greater part of them render the home market of that country of so great extent, as to be alone sufficient to support very great manufactures, and to admit of very considerable subdivisions of labour. The home market of China is, perhaps, in extent, not much inferior to the market of all the different countries of Europe put together. A more extensive foreign trade, however, which to this great home market added the foreign market of all the rest of the world, especially if any considerable part of this trade was carried on in Chinese ships, could scarce fail to increase very much the manufactures of China, and to improve very much the productive powers of its manufacturing industry. By a more extensive navigation, the Chinese would naturally learn the art of using and constructing, themselves, all the different machines made use of in other countries, as well as in the other improvements of art and industry which are practised in all the different parts of the world. Upon their present plan, they have little opportunity of improving themselves by the example of any other nation, expect that of the Japanese.

Smith's emphasis on trade highlights one of the reasons for the deterioration in the Western view of China: the desire for trade with China. At that time trade was restricted to Canton (Guangzhou). The main task of the famous first British Embassy, which Lord George Macartney (1737–1806) led to China in 1793–94, was to negotiate a treaty of commerce and friendship and to establish a resident minister at Emperor Qianlong's court. The embassy failed in that task, but did make more persistent attempts at trade and other dealings later on.

12

MANNERS AND CHARACTER

LORD MACARTNEY

The last major expression of the positive image of China so common in the eighteenth century was through the work of Sir George Leonard Staunton (1737–1801), who wrote the official account of Lord George Macartney's embassy to the Chinese court. Macartney himself wrote a diary and extensive observations about the Chinese. Unlike Staunton's account, which appeared in 1797, Macartney's was not printed in full until 1962, in a version edited by J. L. Cranmer-Byng. Yet it is amusing and perceptive, and generally more interesting than Staunton's work. Macartney is open, honest, and willing to criticize both China and his own society. The following extracts come from the first section of Lord Macartney's observations on China, entitled 'Manners and Character'.

When Marco Polo, the Venetian, visited China in the thirteenth century, it was about the time of the conquest of China by the western or Mongol Tartars, with Kublai Khan, a grandson of Genghis Khan, at their head. A little before that period the Chinese had reached their highest pitch of civilization, and no doubt they were then a very civilized people in comparison of their Tartar conquerors, and their European contemporaries, but not having improved and advanced forward, or having rather gone back, at least for these one hundred and fifty years past, since the last conquest by the northern or Manchu Tartars; while we have been every day rising in arts and sciences, they are actually become a semi-barbarous people in comparison with the present nations of Europe. Hence it is that they retain the vanity, conceit, and pretensions that are usually the concomitants of half-knowledge, and that, though during their intercourse with the embassy they perceived many of the advantages we had over them, they seemed rather surprised than mortified, and sometimes affected not to see what they could not avoid feeling. In their address to strangers they are not restrained by any bashfulness or *mauvaise honte*, but present themselves with an easy confident air, as if they considered themselves the superiors, and that nothing in their manners or appearance could be found defective or inaccurate. . . .

Every Chinese who aspires to preferment attaches himself to some Tartar of consequence, and professes the utmost devotion to his service; but such is the strong and radical dislike in the client to the patron, that scarcely any benefits can remove it and plant gratitude in its place. As the nature of dependence is to grow false, it cannot be wondered at if these Chinese are not strict observers of truth. They have indeed so little idea of its moral obligation, that they promise you everything you desire, without the slightest intention of performance, and then violate their promises without scruple, having had no motive for making them that I could perceive, unless it were that they imagined what they said might be agreeable to you just at the moment. When detected or reproached they make light of the matter themselves, and appear neither surprised nor ashamed; but nevertheless it was evident that they particularly remarked our punctuality and our strict attention to truth in all our transactions with them, and respected us accordingly.

Although the difference of ranks be perhaps more distinctly marked in China than in any other country, yet I often observed that the Mandarins treat their domestic servants with great condescension and talk to them with good nature and familiarity; but in return an unremitted attention and obedience are expected and never withheld.

A Chinese family is regulated with the same regard to subordination and economy that is observed in the government of a state; the paternal authority, though unlimited, is usually exercised with kindness and indulgence. In China children are indeed sometimes sold, and infants exposed by the parents, but only in cases of the most hopeless indigence and misery, when they must inevitably perish if kept at home; but where the thread of attachment is not thus snapped asunder by the anguish of the parent, it every day grows stronger and becomes indissoluble for life.

There is nothing more striking in the Chinese character through all ranks than this most respectable union. Affection and duty walk hand in hand and never desire a separation. The fondness of the father is constantly felt and always increasing; the dependence of the son is perfectly understood by him; he never wishes it to be lessened. . . .

At their meals they use no towels, napkins, table-cloths, flat plates, glasses, knives nor forks, but help themselves with their fingers, or with their chopsticks, which are made of wood or ivory, about six inches long, round and smooth, and not very cleanly. Their meat is served up ready cut in small bowls, each guest having a separate bowl to himself. Seldom above two sit together at the same table, and never above four. They are all foul feeders and eaters of garlic and strong-scented vegetables, and drink mutually out of the same cup which, though sometimes rinsed, is never washed or wiped clean. They use little vinegar, no olive oil, cyder, ale, beer, or grape wine; their chief drink is tea, or liquors distilled or prepared from rice and other vegetables, of different degrees of strength according to their taste, some of which are tolerably agreeable and resemble strong Madeira.

They almost all smoke tobacco and consider it as a compliment to offer each other a whiff of their pipes. They also take snuff, mostly Brazil, but in small quantities, not in that beastly profusion which is often practised in England, even by some of our fine ladies.

They have no water-closets nor proper places of retirement; the necessaries are quite public and open, and the ordure is continually removing from them, which occasions a stench in almost every place one approaches. . . .

The common people of China are a strong hardy race, patient, industrious, and much given to traffic and all the arts of gain; cheerful and loquacious under the severest labour, and by no means that sedate, tranquil people they have been represented. In their joint efforts and exertions they work with incessant vociferation, often angrily scold one another, and seem ready to proceed to blows, but scarcely ever come to that extremity. The inevitable severity of the law restrains them, for the loss of a life is always punished by the death of the offender, even though he acted merely in self-defence, and without any malice prepense.

Superstitious and suspicious in their temper they at first appeared shy and apprehensive of us, being full of prejudices against strangers, of whose cunning and ferocity a thousand ridiculous tales had been propagated, and perhaps industriously encouraged by the government, whose political system seems to be to endeavour to persuade the people that they are themselves already perfect and can therefore learn nothing from others; but it is to little purpose. A nation that does not advance must retrograde, and finally fall back to barbarism and misery.

A Chinese boy who was appointed to wait upon young George Staunton would not for a long time trust himself to sleep in the house with our European servants, being afraid, he said, that they would eat him. The Chinese, however, at all the seaports where we touched were quite free from these foolish notions; and I flatter myself that the Embassy will have effectually removed them in all the provinces which it passed through.

The lower sort most heartily detest the Mandarins and persons in authority, whose arbitrary power of punishing, oppressing, and insulting them they fear, whose injustice they feel, and whose rapacity they must feed. The Mandarins themselves are equally at the mercy of their superiors, the Ministers and Grand Secretaries of the Court, and are punishable by confiscation, and even by death, not only for their own offences, but for what others may do amiss within their department. They are responsible for whatever happens in the place where their authority extends; accident is construed into intention, and unavoidable error into wilful neglect. But this is not all, for the penalty is often inflicted on the offender's whole family, as well as on the offender himself. The Ministers and Grand Secretaries too are liable to any indignity which the caprice of the Emperor may chance to dictate. The bamboo is one of the grand instruments of discipline from which no rank or elevation is exempt or secure. The Emperor's nearest relations, even his own sons, are subject to it, and there are two of them now living upon whom it is well known to have been inflicted. . . .

As my knowledge of the female world in China was very limited, I have little to say upon the subject, but it may not be improper to say that little. The women of the lower sort are much weather-beaten, and by no means handsome. Beauty is soon withered by early and frequent parturition, by hard labour and hard fare. They have however a smart air, which arises from their manner of tying up their hair on the crown of their heads, and interspersing it with flowers and other ornaments. In the neighbourhood of Pekin I met some ladies of the higher ranks in their carriages, who appeared to have fair complexions and delicate features. They were all painted, as indeed are many of the inferior classes.

There is no law to prohibit intermarriages between the Tartars and the Chinese, but they very seldom intermarry. The Manchu and Mongol Tartars chiefly marry together, and scarcely ever with any of the other Tartar tribes. The Manchus often give a large portion with their daughters; the reverse is the case among the Chinese, where the parent usually receives a consideration or handsome present from his son-in-law.

The Tartar ladies have hitherto kept their legs at liberty, and would never submit to the Chinese operation of crippling the feet, though it is said that many of their husbands were desirous of introducing it into their families. I made many inquiries relative to this strange practice, but with little satisfaction. Chou [a constant Chinese companion] admitted that no very good reason could be given for it. Its being an ancient custom was the best he could assign, and he confessed that a religious adherence to ancient customs, without much investigation of their origin, was a principal feature in the Chinese character. He added, however, that it possibly might have taken its rise from oriental jealousy, which had always been ingenious in its contrivances for securing the ladies to their owners; and that certainly a good way of keeping them at home was to make it very troublesome and painful to them to gad abroad. The rendering useless and deformed one part of the human body that is connate with the rest is little less strange than the practice of totally cutting off another; and yet we express no disgust nor surprise at the operation of circumcision, which prevails among a large proportion of mankind, and the Italian opera has long reconciled us to the indecency of castration. . . .

I by no means want to apologise for the Chinese custom of squeezing their womens' pettitoes into the shoes of an infant, which I think an infernal distortion. Yet so much are people subject to be warped and blinded by fashion, that every Chinese above the vulgar considers it as a female accomplishment not to be dispensed with. Nay, a reverend apostolic missionary at Peking assured me that in love affairs the glimpse of a little fairy foot was to a Chinese a most powerful provocative. Perhaps we are not quite free from a little folly of the same kind ourselves. We have not yet indeed pushed it to the extreme the Chinese have done, yet are we such admirers of it, that what with tight shoes, high heels and ponderous buckles, if our ladies' feet are not crippled they are certainly very much contracted, and it is impossible to say where the abridgement will stop. It is not a great many years ago that in England thread-paper waists, steel stays, and tight lacing were in high fashion, and the ladies' shapes were so tapered down from the bosom to the hips that there was some danger of breaking off in the middle upon any exertion. No woman was thought worth having who measured above eighteen inches round at the girdle.

13
A MAXIM FOR TYRANNY

JOHN BARROW

One of Sir George Staunton's assistants in writing his account of the 1793–94 embassy to China was John Barrow (1764–1848). Staunton was Barrow's patron and was largely responsible for getting him to take part in the embassy. He hired him as librarian from 1795 to 1797, but in 1804 Barrow published his own account, which put forward a very different view of China, its government, and its people. Indeed, although Barrow 'respectfully inscribed' his book to Macartney and signed himself as the Earl's 'most faithful and obliged humble servant', he also added an 'advertisement' in which he in effect apologized for his deviance from 'the almost universally received opinion' about China. He meant was that whereas Staunton had been very positive about China, he himself was putting forward a harshly critical view. The following extract shows his views on Chinese government. While Barrow agrees with much eighteenth-century opinion in seeing China as a despotism, he also castigates it as oppressive and malign.

The Emperor being considered as the common father of his people, is accordingly invested with the exercise of the same authority over them, as the father of a family exerts on those of his particular household. In this sense he takes the title of the *Great Father;* and by his being thus placed above any earthly control, he is supposed to be also above earthly descent, and therefore, as a natural consequence, he sometimes styles himself the *sole ruler of the world* and the *Son of Heaven.* . . .

It is greatly to be lamented that a system of government, so plausible in theory, should be liable to so many abuses in practice; and that this fatherly care and affection in the governors, and filial duty and reverence in the governed, would, with much more propriety, be expressed by the terms of tyranny, oppression, and injustice in the one, and by fear, deceit, and disobedience in the other.

The first grand maxim on which the Emperor acts is seldom to appear before the public, a maxim whose origin would be difficultly traced to any principle of affection or solicitude for his children; much more easily explained as the offspring of suspicion. The tyrant who may be conscious of having committed, or assented to, acts of cruelty and oppression, must feel a reluctance to mix with those who may have smarted under the lash of his power, naturally concluding that some secret hand may be led, by a single blow, to avenge his own wrongs, or those of his fellow-subjects. The principle, however, upon which the Emperor of China seldom shews himself in public, and then only in the height of splendour and magnificence, seems to be established on a policy of a very different kind to that of self-preservation. A power that acts in secret, and whose influence is felt near and remote at the same moment, makes a stronger impression on the mind, and is regarded with more dread and awful respect, than if the agent was always visible and familiar to the eye of every one.

PART VI

IMPERIALISM GATHERS MOMENTUM

Western views of China remained largely negative throughout the nineteenth century, when the West gained enormous confidence through the Industrial Revolution and spread its power and influence throughout the world. China, on the other hand, had reached its apogee of power and prosperity in the eighteenth century and by the middle of the nineteenth century was in rapid decline. The clearest sign of this was the outbreak of insurrections, the most devastating being the Taiping Rebellion, which shook the whole country, especially the south, from 1851 to 1864.

Britain and France were the most important sources of Western views about China. For the first time, however, we find the rise of the United States as a major source of such views. Indeed, some of the most important writers of the century on China were Americans, perhaps the most obvious example being Samuel Wells Williams.

14
CHINA'S ARISTOCRACY

EVARISTE RÉGIS HUC

TRANSLATED BY COLIN MACKERRAS

*A most significant Western observer of China in the second half of the
nineteenth century was Evariste Régis Huc (1813–60), a French missionary
of the Vincentian order who lived and travelled many years in China. He
was among one of the few Westerners of his time to go to Tibet, reaching
Lhasa early in 1846.*

*Huc's views on China are contained in his two-volume work, L'empire
chinois, first published in Paris in 1854. Although some aspects of China
impressed Huc favourably, the tone of his work is sharply critical. He
praises China's education system, and the following passage describes
members of the aristocracy who paid him a visit while he was travelling in
Sichuan Province.*

While we were living as missionaries we were most often in
contact with the lower classes; in the countryside with
peasants and in the towns with the artisans, since, in
China as everywhere, it is among the people that Christianity
strikes root first. We were happy for this opportunity to get to know
the aristocracy of this curious nation. Well brought up Chinese are
truly amiable and their society has many charms. Their politeness
is neither tiring nor tedious, as one might imagine. There is
something exquisite in it, even natural, and it has none of that
affectation which one finds among those who pretend to elegance
but don't understand the customs of the world. The conversation
of the Chinese is sometimes very spiritual. The excessive
compliments and words of praise which one is supposed to say to
each other can, when one is not used to it, be irritating and tiring.

But even then there is so much good grace that one readily gets accustomed to it.

Among these visitors there was especially a group of young people who amazed us. Their demeanour was unreservedly modest. There was a mixture of modesty and confidence which harmonized delightfully with their youth. They spoke but little and only when asked a question. While their elders were talking they were content to take part in the conversation only by facial expression and gracious head movements. Their fans and the way they handled them only served to add to the satisfactions of this Chinese society. We were hard put to prove to this elegant aristocracy that French urbanity could equal the ceremonious politeness of the Chinese.

In contrast to the above, Huc has some very caustic remarks to make on the prevalence of opium, and his detailed views on the position of women in society are bleak and condemnatory. He believes the only discernible improvements for women are due to Christianity and the missionaries who brought it.

The condition of the Chinese woman is pitiable. Suffering, privation, contempt, misery, and degradation are her lot from the cradle to the grave. For a start, her birth is generally seen as a humiliation and dishonour for the family; it is evidence of a curse from heaven. If she is not promptly suffocated, according to an atrocious custom discussed later, she is considered and treated like a creature of utterly contemptible condition and hardly belonging to the human race. This idea seems so beyond doubt that Pan-houi-pan [Ban Zhao, first century AD], a famous woman among Chinese writers, goes out of her way to humiliate her own sex by incessantly recalling the low rank which women occupy in creation: 'When a boy is born', she says, 'he sleeps on a bed, he is dressed in robes, and plays with pearls; everybody runs to obey his cries as if they were those of a prince. But when a girl is born, she sleeps on the ground, covered with a simple sheet, she plays with tiles, she cannot do either good or bad, but must think only of getting the wine and food, and not annoying her parents.' . . .

Part of a Bridal Procession en Route to the House of the Bridegroom on the Wedding-Day, a nineteenth-century view of a wedding in South China. Source: Reverend Justus Doolittle, *Social Life of the Chinese*.

Polygamy, which is allowed to the Chinese, simply increases the misfortune and miseries of a married woman. When she has ceased to be young, if she cannot have children or has given no son to the head of the family, he takes a second wife, to whom the first becomes in effect a servant. Constant warfare then prevails in the household; one witnesses nothing but jealousy, animosity, quarrels, and often even battles. Only when they are alone are they allowed on occasion to brood on their sorrows in peace and cry their eyes out on the incurable miseries of their hapless fate.

This permanent state of degradation and misery to which women are reduced can sometimes push them to appalling extremities. The judicial ostentations of China are often filled with events which stretch to the last limits of tragedy. The number of women who hang themselves or commit suicide in various ways is very substantial. When such an event occurs in a family, the husband is desolated, as well he might be; for he has of course suddenly sustained a considerable loss, and here he is facing the need to buy another wife.

It is understandable that the hard lot of poor Chinese women must be much better in Christian families. . . .

The rehabilitation of women operates slowly in China, it is true, but it is nevertheless striking and effective. For a start, in Christian families, the little girl who has just come into the world cannot be sacrificed as among the pagans. Religion watches over her birth, takes her into its arms with love, and says, showing her to her parents: 'Here is a baby girl created in the image of God and destined like you to immortality. Thank the Heavenly Father for giving her to you, and may the Queens of the Angels be her patron.' . . .

It is above all in the Christian marriage that the Chinese woman shakes off the frightful servitude of pagan morals and enters the great human family with her rights and privileges. It is true that the force of prejudice and habit still does not always allow her to express her inclinations openly and choose herself the one who will share her joys and sorrows in this life. Yet her wishes do count for something and, more than once, we have seen a young woman, through energetic resistance, force her parents to break engagements contracted without consulting her.[1]

15

NO VALUE IN TRUTH

R. K. DOUGLAS

One of the great accomplishments of the West in the nineteenth century was the acceleration in the compilation of enormous encyclopedias. At the peak of these stands the Encyclopædia Britannica, of which the fourth to the ninth editions were published in the nineteenth century. It is likely that, in relation to all sources, the encyclopedia was most influential in the nineteenth century, with the prestige of the Encyclopædia Britannica being the greatest of all, certainly in the English-speaking world.

The author of the entry on China in the ninth edition was R. K. Douglas, Professor of Chinese at King's College, London. The British had learned a great deal about China since beginning their missionary endeavours and imperialist exploits there. Douglas's entry is thus enormously scholarly, detailed, and comprehensive, with much attention given to physical features, history, language, literature, government, society, religion, and other factors. At the same time, in accordance with the times, there is a certain feeling that the author regards his subject as an inferior civilization.

The following is extracted from Douglas's views on Chinese government and law.

The government may be described as a patriarchal despotism. The emperor is the father of his people, and as a father is responsible for the training and behaviour of his children, receiving blame when they prove unworthy, and reward when they show themselves to be virtuous; so is the people's welfare the emperor's first care, and their preservation from all harm, both moral and physical, his first duty. When the people become unruly the emperor views their conduct as the result of his own negligence or want of wisdom, and when peace prevails he accepts it as the consequence of his fatherly solicitude and care. Like a father also, he holds autocratic sway over his household—the empire. In his hand lies the power of life and death. Whom he will he slays, and whom he will he keeps alive. But there is a limit to his absolutism. The duties attaching to the relations existing between emperor and people are reciprocal; and, while it is the duty of the subject to render willing and submissive obedience to the sovereign so long as his rule is just and beneficent, it is also incumbent on him to resist his authority so soon as he ceases to be a minister of God for good. This sacred right of rebellion was distinctly taught by Confucius, and was emphasized by Mencius, who went the length of asserting that a ruler who, by the practice of injustice and oppression, had forfeited his right to rule, should not only be dethroned, but might, if circumstances required it, be put to death. . . .

Theoretically the system of government in the provinces is excellent, but as a matter of fact it is corrupt to the core. Several causes have tended to bring about this disastrous state of things. In the first place, the mandarins, even when they receive their salaries, which is by no means always the case, are so wretchedly underpaid that the money they receive from this source is barely sufficient to support the staff which it is necessary for them to maintain. . . . The consequence is that, as few mandarins have private means, they are obliged to supplement their official incomes by illegal exactions and bribes. And this evil is further heightened by the regulation which forbids that a mandarin should hold any office for more than three years. It becomes the selfish interest, therefore, of every office-holder to get as much out of the people within his jurisdiction as he possibly can in that time. The instant he arrives at his post it is customary for all the subordinate officials to pay their respects to him, on which occasion they are expected to display their loyalty by offering presents of more or less value according to the means at their command. No subaltern dare absent himself, being perfectly aware that such an omission of duty would deprive him of all hope of promotion, and would subject him on the slightest pretence, or even without any pretence whatever, to official persecution and ruin. . . .

As may readily be imagined, this corruption in high places has a most demoralizing effect on the people generally. Dishonesty prevails to a frightful extent, and with it, of course, untruthfulness. The Chinese set little or no value upon truth, and thus some slight excuse is afforded for the use of torture in their courts of justice;

for it is argued that where the value of an oath is not understood, some other means must be resorted to to extract evidence, and the readiest means to hand is doubtless torture. The kind most commonly inflicted is flogging. The obdurate witness is laid flat on his face, and the executioner delivers his blows on the upper part of the thighs with the concave side of a split bamboo, the sharp edges of which mutilate the sufferer terribly. The punishment is continued until the man either supplies the evidence required or becomes insensible. . . .

It is only natural to expect that in a country where the torture of witnesses is permitted, the punishments inflicted on the guilty should exceed in cruelty, and this is eminently the case in China. The Mongolian race is confessedly obtuse-nerved and insensible to suffering, and no doubt Chinese culprits do not suffer nearly as much as members of more sensitive races would under similar treatment. But even granting this, the refined cruelties perpetrated by Chinamen on Chinamen admit of no apology.

A NEED FOR CHRISTIANITY

SAMUEL WELLS WILLIAMS

The Protestant missionaries of the nineteenth century produced some authors who wrote extensively on China: both general works painting a broad picture of the country and its people and narrower accounts of Chinese society, including its religion and festivals. On the whole they were censorious of China and, in line with the very reason they were there, recomended solutions to social ills through the adoption of Christianity.

Possibly the greatest of these missionaries was the American Samuel Wells Williams (1812–84). He lived over forty years in China, arriving in Guangzhou in 1833 and, after returning home, became Professor of Chinese Language and Literature at Yale College. He compiled dictionaries of Chinese tones and syllables, but his major work was The Middle Kingdom, *probably the greatest compendium of knowledge about China produced in the nineteenth century. First published in 1848, it was thoroughly revised for republication in 1883, by which time Williams knew far more about his subject. Extraordinarily broad in its approach, the book covers themes as far apart as natural history, political history, population, government, law, social life, and literature. Having dedicated so much of his life to converting China to Christianity, he appreciated much about the Chinese and puts himself forward as their friend. In the 1883 edition he writes that 'I have endeavored to show the better traits of their national character'. Conversely, his overall tone and attitude towards China, its institutions, and people is condescending and often harsh. His extremely caustic comment on the Chinese character has been quoted frequently,[2] and needs no repetition here.*

In justifying his lengthy stay in China and his thorough study of its civilization, Williams has the following to say at the beginning of the 1883 edition of his great work.

I ts civilization has been developed under its own institutions; its government has been modelled without knowledge or reference to that of any other kingdom; its literature has borrowed nothing from the genius or research of the scholars of other lands; its language is unique in its symbols, its structure, and its antiquity; its inhabitants are remarkable for their industry, peacefulness, numbers, and peculiar habits. The examination of such a people, and so extensive a country, can hardly fail of being both instructive and entertaining, and if rightly pursued, lead to a stronger conviction of the need of the precepts and sanctions of the Bible to the highest development of every nation in its personal, social, and political relations in this world, as well as to individual happiness in another. It is to be hoped, too, that at this date in the world's history, there are many more than formerly, who desire to learn the conditions and wants of others, not entirely for their own amusement and congratulations at their superior knowledge and advantages, but also to promote the well-being of their fellow-men, and impart liberally of the gifts they themselves enjoy. Those who desire to do this, will find that few families of mankind are more worthy of their greatest efforts than those comprised within the limits of the Chinese Empire; while none stand in more need of the purifying, ennobling, and invigorating principles of our holy religion to develop and enforce their own theories of social improvement.

Williams shows the difference between good precepts and reality in the following discussion of official corruption.

When one is living in the country itself, to hear the complaints of individuals against the extortion and cruelty of their rulers, and to read the reports of judicial murder, torture, and crime in the *Peking Gazette*, are enough to cause one to wonder how such atrocities and oppressions are endured from year to year, and why the sufferers do not rise and throw aside the tyrannous power which thus abuses them. But the people are generally conscious that their rulers are no better than themselves, and that they would really gain nothing by such a procedure, and their desire to maintain as great a degree of peace as possible leads them to submit to many evils, which in western countries would soon be remedied or cause a revolution. . . .

One mode taken by the highest ranks to obtain money is to notify inferiors that there are certain days on which presents are expected, and custom soon increases these as much as the case will admit. Subscriptions for objects of public charity or disbursements, such as an inundation, a bad harvest, bursting of dikes, and other similar things which the government must look after, are not unfrequently made a source of revenue to the incumbents by requiring much more than is needed; those who subscribe are rewarded by an empty title, a peacock's feather, or employment in some insignificant formality. The sale of titular rank is a source of revenue, but the government never attempts to subvert or interfere with the well-known channel of attaining office by literary merit, and it seldom confers much real power for money when unconnected with some degree of fitness. The security of its own position is not to be risked for the sake of an easy means of filling its exchequer, yet it is impossible to say how far the sale of office and title is carried. The censors inveigh against it, and the Emperor almost apologizes for resorting to it, but it is nevertheless constantly practised.

17
CHINA FINDS A DEFENDER

THOMAS TAYLOR MEADOWS

*While the dominant perception of China in the nineteenth century was very
negative, there were important writers who defended China. One was
Thomas Taylor Meadows, an official interpreter in the British civil service,
who had begun to learn Chinese in the early 1840s at the University of
Munich. Although parts of his book,* The Chinese and their Rebellions,
*present hideous images of the country, the overall thrust is quite positive.
Just as importantly, he devotes considerable space to attacking works
which put the Chinese in what he considers an unreasonably bad light. In
particular, he devotes a chapter to attacking the works of Huc. The civil war
mentioned is the Taiping Rebellion, which ravaged China from 1851 until
1864. The Manchoo government was the Qing dynasty, ruled by the
Manchus, who had taken over China in 1644.*

No people, whether of ancient or modern times, has
possessed a Sacred Literature so completely exempt as the
Chinese from licentious descriptions, and from every
offensive expression. There is not a single sentence in the whole of
the Sacred Books and their annotations that may not, when
translated word for word, be read aloud in any family circle in
England. Again, in every other non-Christian country, idolatry has
been associated with human sacrifices and with the deification of
vice, accompanied by licentious rites and orgies. Not a sign of all
this exists in China. Idolatry is endured by Confucianism as a
superstition; but immoral ceremonies are prohibited, and not a
single indecent idol is exposed in any of the numerous temples in
the country. . . .

In closing this subject, I must once again warn the reader against
believing the ridiculously exaggerated descriptions given forth by
some writers of every bad feature that they could detect in Chinese

In Daoist ceremonies for the dead, it was the custom for priests to chant
mourning laments accompanied by cymbals. They turned a 'bridge-ladder' which
contained lamps and, at the top, a candle. After death all was darkness, a result
of which the spirit of the deceased required lighting to guide it on its way. This is
a nineteenth-century view of such a ceremony, with the corpse on the left.
Source: Reverend Justus Doolittle, *Social Life of the Chinese.*

life. Civil war has of late years let loose passions, which are in
happier times restrained by their national morality; and the
Manchoo government is exciting in the West a feeling of
astonishment and horror by its indiscriminate executions of
thousands of rebel prisoners. But this is done in flagrant violation
of the principles of Chinese polity. And I venture to say, that even
now the Chinese are nowhere what they are represented as having
been a few years ago in M. Huc's *Chinese Empire.* For instance, M.
Huc broadly asserts that the birth of a daughter 'is in general
regarded as a humiliation and dishonor for the family; it is a
manifest proof of a curse of heaven'. *Can* any English fathers and
mothers believe that? I have seen hundreds of fathers walking
about with such little dishonors and curses in their arms,
handsomely dressed and prattling away to the pleased and proud
papas.

18
THE SMALL-FOOTED CLASS

JUSTUS DOOLITTLE

*The distinguished Protestant missionary Reverend Justus Doolittle
(1824–80) worked in Fuzhou, the capital of Fujian Province, and wrote a
series of letters about China. From 1861 to 1864 these letters were
published anonymously, under the title 'Jottings about the Chinese', in the
Hong Kong newspaper* China Mail. *On returning to the United States,
Doolittle republished these letters, along with other material, in his two-
volume* Social Life of the Chinese.

*Doolittle was among several nineteenth-century Western writers to
tackle the problem of female infanticide. The reference to 'the small-footed
class' is clearly to the practice of foot-binding. In his long treatment of this
subject, Doolittle remarks that 'small feet are a mark, not of wealth, for the
poorest families sometimes have their daughter's feet bandaged—it is
rather an index of gentility. It is the fashionable form.' It is in this context
that his use of the term 'class' is to be taken.*

Female Infanticide

No doubt infanticide is more common in some localities
and provinces than in others. But . . . there are most
indubitable reasons for believing that it is extensively
practised at this place [Fuzhou] and in the neighbouring districts,
and also that it is tolerated by the government, and that the subject
is treated with indifference and with shocking levity by the mass. . . .

The principal methods of depriving the unfortunates of life are
three: by drowning in a tub of water, by throwing into some
running stream, or by burying alive. The latter method is affirmed
to be selected by a few families in the country under the belief that
their next child will, in consequence, be a boy. The most common

五子日昇

A print of a lucky charm showing baby boys, the message being that the greatest fortune is to be had by a large number of sons. Source: Henri Doré, SJ, *Researches into Chinese Superstitions.*

way is the first mentioned. The person who usually performs the murderous act is the father of the child. Midwives and personal friends generally decline it as being none of their business, and as affording an occasion for blame or unpleasant reflection in future years. Generally the mother prefers the child should be given away to being destroyed. Sometimes, however, the parents agree to destroy rather than give away their infant daughter, in order to keep it from a life of poverty or shame.

The professed reason for the destruction of female infants by poor people is their poverty. For an indigent labouring man to support a family of girls, and to marry them off according to custom, is regarded as an impossibility. In the country, girls and women of the large-footed class work in the fields like boys and men. In the city and suburbs, females are kept much more at home, especially those belonging to the small-footed class. They are generally able to get indoor employment from shop-keepers. At the time girls are married, an amount of furniture and clothing must be furnished them as outfit or dowry by their parents, which the poor are really unable to afford. When married, a daughter is reckoned as belonging to another family, and neither she nor her husband is expected to afford pecuniary aid to her father or her mother to any great extent. . . .

Poverty is no excuse for the drowning of the female children of the rich. But that infanticide is practised quite frequently by wealthy families rests on the most explicitly and ample testimony, the observation and the admission of their neighbours and their countrymen. . . .

The rich here usually destroy the girls born to them after they have the number they wish to keep and rear. Boys, on the other hand, are always considered a valuable addition to the family. The proportion of instances of infanticide is probably considerably smaller among the wealthy than among the indigent Chinese, for they are not *compelled* (to adopt the language of this people) to destroy their female offspring by the want of means of subsistence. This circumstance makes their crime the more aggravated and inexcusable, for it is perpetrated in cold blood and with determination, without any reason or excuse, *except that they do not wish to rear them!* . . .

The crime of female infanticide is often mentioned with levity by the common people. When seriously appealed to on the subject, though, all deprecate it as contrary to the dictates of reason and the instincts of nature, many are ready boldly to apologize for it, and declare it to be necessary, especially in the families of the excessively poor. While 'it is not, in fact, directly sanctioned by the government, or agreeable to the general spirit of the laws and the institutions of the empire', yet it is tolerated and acquiesced in by the mandarins. No measures are ever taken to find out and punish the murderers of their own infants. Occasionally proclamations are issued by mandarins forbidding the drowning of girls; nevertheless, the crime is extensively practiced with impunity.

In China the doctrine of filial piety is highly lauded, and children of both sexes are required by law and by the usages of society to render the most implicit and even abject deference to the will of their parents. But parents are permitted to discriminate between the sex of their helpless offspring, destroying the female *ad libitum,* and lavishing on the male their care and love. How singularly and emphatically are they 'without natural affection' as regards this subject!

19

CHINESE PARSIMONY

A. H. SMITH

Another in the line of nineteenth-century Protestant missionaries was A. H. Smith (1845–1932), whose Chinese Characteristics remains among the most famous treatments of its subject. The book was first published in 1890 and popularity carried it to a fifth revised edition within a decade. The title page of this fifth edition states that Smith had already been 'twenty-two years a missionary of the American Board in China'.

Smith writes in a confident, amusing style. His command of his subject is evident from the many personal experiences he cites. Although he has the somewhat condescending attitude which marked his age in terms of Western opinion about the Chinese, many of the 'characteristics' are good, and in general Smith seems well disposed towards his subject. The first, and presumably the most important, of the 'characteristics' is 'face', followed by 'economy', or the ability to make do with little, an extract concerning which is given below.

One of the 'Chinese characteristics' to which Smith refers is 'the absence of nerves'; reference is made to it in the extract below. Smith claims that the Chinese are better able to endure pain than Westerners, because of their lack of nerves. 'Occidentals cannot fail to sympathize with the distinguished French lady who sent word to a caller that she "begged to be excused, as she was engaged in dying". In China such an excuse would never be offered, nor, if it were offered, would it be accepted.'

The word 'economy' signifies the rule by which the house should be ordered, especially with reference to the relation between expenditure and income. Economy, as we understand the term, may be displayed in three several ways: by limiting the number of wants, by preventing waste, and by the adjustment of forces in such a manner as to make a little represent a great deal. In each of these ways the Chinese are pre-eminently economical.

One of the first things which impress the traveller in China is the extremely simple diet of the people. The vast bulk of the population seems to depend upon a few articles, such as rice, beans in various preparations, millet, garden vegetables, and fish. These, with a few other things, form the staple of countless millions, supplemented it may be on the feast-days, or other special occasions, with a bit of meat.

Now that so much attention is given in Western lands to the contrivance of ways in which to furnish nourishing food to the very poor, at a minimum cost, it is not without interest to learn the undoubted fact that, in ordinary years, it is in China quite possible to furnish wholesome food in abundant quantity at a cost for each adult of not more than two cents a day. Even in famine times, thousands of persons have been kept alive for months on an allowance of not more than a cent and a half a day. This implies the general existence in China of a high degree of skill in the preparation of food. Poor and coarse as their food often is, insipid and even repulsive as it not infrequently seems to the foreigner, it is impossible not to recognize the fact that, in the cooking and serving of what they have, the Chinese are past-masters of the culinary art. . . .

Many of the fruits of Chinese economy are not at all pleasing to the Westerners, but we cannot help admitting the genuine nature of the claim which may be built on them. In parts of the Empire, especially (strange to say) in the north, the children of both sexes roam around in the costume of the Garden of Eden, for many months of the year. This comes to be considered more comfortable for them, but the primary motive is economy. The stridulous squeak of the vast army of Chinese wheelbarrows is due to the absence of the few drops of oil which might stop it, but which never do stop it, because to those who are gifted with 'an absence of nerves' the squeak is cheaper than the oil.

If a Japanese emigrates, it is specified in his contract that he is to be furnished daily with so many gallons of hot water, in which he may, according to custom, parboil himself. The Chinese have their bathing-houses too, but the greater part of the Chinese people never go near them, nor indeed ever saw one. 'Do you wash your child every day?' said an inquisitive foreign lady to a Chinese mother, who was seen throwing shovelfuls of dust over her progeny, and then wiping it off with an old broom. 'Wash him every day!' was the indignant response; 'he was never washed since he was born!' To the Chinese generally, the motto could never be made even intelligible which was put in his window by a dealer in soap, 'Cheaper than dirt.'

20
THE SCOURGE OF OPIUM

W. A. P. MARTIN

An American missionary who lived most of the second half of the nineteenth century in China was W. A. P. Martin (1827–1916). Apart from his missionary work, both the Chinese and American governments used his services for teaching, diplomacy, and other purposes. Martin wrote extensively about Chinese society, both of the north and south. The preface to his study A Cycle of Cathay, *published in 1900, expresses to former Chinese students the opinion that they would 'find in it the same sympathetic appreciation of their country and the same candour of criticism which, I am sure, they have learned to expect'.*

In the following passage, Martin discusses his sorrow at the prevalence of opium, the consumption of which gathered momentum while he was in China. He also puts forward suggestions for curing this terrible evil.

I began to study the effects of opium-smoking, nor was it possible to dismiss the subject as long as I remained in China. The conclusion to which I was brought is that to the Chinese the practice is an unmitigated curse. Whether it is worse than the abuse of alcohol among us I shall not undertake to decide. The contrast between the effects of the two drugs is remarkable. Liquor makes a man noisy and furious; opium makes him quiet and rational. The drinker commits crime when he has too much; the opium-smoker when he has too little. Drinking is a social vice, and drunkenness a public nuisance; opium-smoking is mostly a private vice, indulged at home; but even in opium-shops it is more offensive to the nose than to the eye or ear. Alcohol imprints on the face a fiery glow; opium, an ashy paleness. Alcoholic drinks bloat and fatten; opium emaciates. A drunkard may work well if kept from his cups; an opium-smoker is good for nothing until he has had his pipe. A drunkard can in most cases cure himself by force of will; the opium habit is a disease, which to break from requires, in all cases, the help of medicine. It takes years for alcohol to reduce a man to slavery; opium rivets its fetters in a few weeks or months. It does not take the place of tobacco, which, used by all classes as a more or less innocent indulgence, is indispensable to the opium-smoker; nor does it take the place of alcoholic drinks, which are consumed as much as ever. Even its moderate use unfits a man for most pursuits. A thousand opium-smokers were at one time dismissed from the army as disqualified for service. In the long run, the insidious drug saps the strength, stupefies the mind, and of course shortens the span of life. Its expense, though great in the aggregate, is nothing in comparison with the loss of time and energy sure to follow in its wake. . . .

Many a bright student have I seen ruined by opium-smoking. In the earlier stages of the habit it is usually impossible to detect, but at length it reveals itself. One who was sent to France as interpreter to the Chinese envoy smoked himself to death as a relief from family troubles. When near his end he said his opium-pipe was his only consolation—*Mon plaisir unique*, he called it. Another, emaciated and sallow when he went to Russia, came back after some years fat and flourishing. He explained to me that the change was due to the giving up of opium, which, said he, 'I was obliged to forego, because it was not to be had.' At first the pipe is sought as a source of enjoyment, or an incentive to the passions; in later stages it is taken as a relief from pain. . . .

Missionaries, who see its ravages among the people, all denounce it. Chinese officers have of late made spasmodic attempts to save portions of their people from the rising flood. General Tso [Zuo Zongtang] forbade the cultivation of the poppy in the Northwest and destroyed the crops. . . . Had the mandarins acted in concert, they might have suppressed the vice even after the legalization of the import; but they never pull together for any public purpose whatever. It is now too late. The native drug amounts to five or ten times the foreign, and the foreign trade is falling off. It is significant that Japan strictly prohibits the use of opium, having before her eyes such an object-lesson as China. . . .

What proportion of the people are infected it is impossible to say, as it varies from district to district—some kind of local option keeping the poison out of certain places, while in others, especially where the drug is grown, its pallid mark is seen on every face, not even women being exempt. A few native religious societies are operating against the evil, but the flood continues to rise. The best hope for checking it—though, we fear, a forlorn hope—is in the growing influence of the church of Christ. With the spread of Christianity a healthier moral sentiment will be awakened, which will become effective far beyond the pale of the churches.

PART VII

LAST YEARS OF THE MANCHU

By the end of the nineteenth century, China seemed helpless. Many in the West, including those who felt kindly towards it, believed that the Chinese empire was about to fall apart. The summer of 1900 saw the rebels known as Boxers pour into Beijing. It also saw a coalition of eight powers, all Western but Japan, send their troops into China to suppress these ragged peasants. The seven Western powers were Britain, the United States, France, Germany, Italy, Austria–Hungary, and Russia. This was the only time in history that these powers had united against a common enemy, for normally they were at each others' throats.

While the Manchu dynasty was at an exceedingly low ebb at the time, it did not fall apart. The Manchus lasted for another decade, their dynasty finally being overthrown at the end of 1911.

21

A CENTURY ENDS

CHARLES BERESFORD

The following account is by a British aristocrat, Rear-Admiral Lord Charles Beresford, MP (1846–1919). At the behest of the Associated Chambers of Commerce of Great Britain, Beresford made a visit to China which lasted from late 1898 to early 1899. His mission was to advise on the wisdom of investing capital in trade enterprise in China and on other matters affecting British trade there. In other words, Beresford's visit took place just after the so-called 'scramble for the concessions' which had resulted in the lease of the Hong Kong New Territories to Britain for ninety-nine years, and just before the outbreak of the Boxer rebellion in Beijing.

In reviewing this Report, several points become apparent:

1. The anxiety of British merchants in China as to the security of capital already invested.
2. The immediate necessity for some assurance to be given to those who are willing to invest further capital.
3. That this existing sense of insecurity is due to the effete condition of the Chinese Government, its corruption, and poverty; and to the continual riots, disturbances, and rebellions throughout the country.
4. That the rapidly advancing disintegration of the Chinese Empire is also due to the pressure of foreign claims, which she has no power either to resist or refuse; all this leading to the total internal collapse of authority.
5. The terrible prospect of a civil revolution, extending over an area as large as Europe amongst 400 millions of people, upon which catastrophe the thin line of European civilization on the coast, and a few ships of war, would have little or no effect.

6. The uncertainty as to what Government would follow, should the present dynasty fall, and our ignorance as to what policy any future Administration would adopt respecting the contracts and concessions made by the existing Tsung-li Yamen [Foreign Ministry].

7. The fear of the traders of all nations in China, that the home Governments of Europe, in their desire to conciliate the interests of those who seek trade with those who want territory, should drift into the 'Sphere of Influence' policy, thereby endangering the expansion of trade, incurring the risk of war, and hastening the partition and downfall of the Chinese Empire.

8. The apprehension existing in all capable minds in China, lest the Governments of Europe, after beginning with the bullying expedient of claims and counter-claims, and then drifting into the policy of 'Spheres of Influence,' should end by hopelessly blocking the 'Open Door'. . . .

With respect to Point 4, I feel most strongly that the pride and profession of Great Britain, to be the champion and chivalrous protector of weak nations, have been humbled and exposed, by her acquiescing and taking part in the disintegrating policy of claims and counter-claims, with which the Chinese Empire is being bullied whilst she is down. I hold that to break up a dismasted craft, the timbers of which are stout and strong, is the policy of the wrecker for his own gain. The real seaman tows her into dock, and refits her for another cruise.

22

THE CRUEL CHINESE

SARAH PIKE CONGER

Mr E. H. Conger, head of the American Legation in China during the first years of the twentieth century, witnessed the Boxer Uprising. He saw large numbers of Chinese peasants besiege the foreign legations and the response of the powers in sending in a united force to relieve the siege. His wife Sarah, a voluminous letter writer, set down her ideas in the many letters she wrote home from China, which were later published. The following are extracts from a particularly long letter she wrote to a nephew, dated 12 December 1900. Despite its lurid descriptions of Chinese cruelties to Christians, it also shows a tolerant attitude towards the Chinese and an awareness of why they could be so hostile to foreigners.

There are most heartrending accounts coming to us of the fate of the missionaries in Paoting [Baoding] Fu and other parts of the interior. When the enraged brute propensities dominate man's intelligence, they make a hell of suffering. In some instances the Boxers took these Christian martyrs and tied one foot to one hand, hung them on a pole, and two men carried them about. At times they would tie their two feet and their two hands together and men would carry them hanging on a pole. One set of Boxers under orders to kill, would take them a long distance, then tell them, 'We have orders to kill you, but we can't do it. We will let you go and look out for yourselves.' Soon another set of Boxers would overtake them; then followed more travel and persecution. Others were disgracefully and cruelly treated, then slashed and beheaded with shameful ceremonies of savagery. Some were fastened in their homes, then the buildings were set on fire. No one was allowed to escape from the consuming flames. These are only illustrations of the most horrible treatment given the foreign Christians.

The native converts received, if possible, even worse treatment. An illustration of the superstitious fear of the Boxers is shown in the case of a child of four years. Little Paul Wang, a child of one of the native Christians, had two sword wounds, one spear wound, and was thrown into the fire three times. He manifested such tenacity of life that the leading Boxers bowed to him, and turned him over to the village elders, saying that Buddha was protecting him. Is it strange that human indignation cries out in its agony for bloodshed in return for these horrible outrages? But the Christian heart knows that the eternal, immutable law of justice prevails. 'Vengeance is mine, I will repay, saith the Lord.' But, oh, how our hearts ache! . . .

I have much sympathy for the Chinese, and yet I do not in any way uphold them nor excuse them in their fiendish cruelty. They have given the foreigner the most sorrowful, most degrading, and most revengeful treatment that their fiendish ideas can conceive. But the facts remain the same: China belongs to the Chinese, and she never wanted the foreigner upon her soil. The foreigner would come, force his life upon the Chinese, and here and there break a cog of the wheels that run their Government so systematically. Even if we grant that China's condition has been improved by these invasions, what right has the foreigner to enter this domain unbidden and unwelcomed? The foreigner has forced himself, his country, his habits, and his productions upon China, always against a strong protest. It kept getting worse for China, and she recognized the fact. At length, in one last struggle, she rose in her mistaken might to wipe the foreigner and his influence from her land. Could we, after taking these facts home to ourselves, blame the Chinese for doing what they could to get rid of what they considered an obnoxious pest that was undermining the long-established customs of their entire country? Their methods, however, are most lamentable. It seems to have been the thought from the beginning of this Chinese uprising to wipe out completely the foreigner and all his invading thoughts and works. The Chinese seemed willing to make untold sacrifices to accomplish this end.

23

RICE CHRISTIANS AND MISSIONARIES

MARSHALL BROOMHALL

Although missionaries loomed large as commentators on China in the nineteenth century, they also had a good deal to say of their own activities, successes, and failures. Not surprisingly, they are generally positive about themselves, and also about their own converts in China. In particular, they are rather keen to defend their converts against the accusation of being simply 'rice Christians', that is, those who turn to Christianity for the material benefits it brings them.

The missionaries had a difficult time in the nineteenth century; the climax came with the Boxer Uprising of 1900, which saw officially sponsored persecution of Christianity. The China Inland Mission, set up in 1865, was among the British Protestant missionary societies to operate in China. Reverend Marshall Broomhall, one of its most important members and a contributor to its early history, wrote of the rebellion as 'the Boxer madness of 1900' and 'the climax of China's anti-foreign policy'. He blamed the Empress Dowager as the source of this anti-foreign policy, whose 'series of denunciatory edicts, marked with bitterness and hate' had helped to stir up the anti-foreign feeling which exploded into the Boxer rebellion. Broomhall reports that 135 of the Mission's members and fifty-three of their children were killed.

Yet in the period following the suppression of the Boxers, Broomhall was happy to report a revival in the fortunes of the Protestant missionaries. He clearly believed this to be a reaction against the Boxers, showing that the average person was supporting not the insane Boxers but the foreign missionaries. Ironically, he even acknowledges 'temporal benefit' on the part of those who professed Christianity. The following passage comes from his history of the Mission's first fifty years.

During the period of transition . . . mass movements towards Christianity began to manifest themselves in different parts of China, and these were followed by a wave of spiritual revival which swept over many of the Churches of the land. So widespread and general were the movements of those days that it is not possible to describe the experiences of one Mission without the use of general terms, for all Missions more or less participated and became mutual helpers one of another. The work of God is one, and when God's Spirit is poured forth this unity or common participation in blessing is felt by all.

It was during the year 1902 that the mass movements were first noticed, especially in Szechwan [Sichuan]. Like the prodigal son in the parable, who was moved by hunger to think of his father's home, many of those who at this time professed an interest in Christianity, did so with the hope of temporal benefit. The collapse of the Boxer movement had demonstrated the might of foreign nations, and many therefore sought the friendship of the foreigner, especially those who desired to escape the unrighteous fleecing of rapacious officials, or assistance in lawsuits with Roman Catholics. Considerable discussion arose among the missionaries as to what was the correct attitude to adopt towards these

A peasant ploughing with a domesticated buffalo in the nineteenth century.
Source: Reverend Justus Doolittle, *Social Life of the Chinese.*

movements; some thought it their duty to let them alone as unspiritual; while others, fully recognizing the ulterior motives, regarded them as God-given opportunities. Wealthy Chinese in many centres were subscribing large sums of money for the opening of Gospel halls, and the questions which had to be faced were, Shall these halls be left to themselves no matter what evil consequences follow? or, Shall they be utilized and the movement controlled and guided?

In many stations the missionaries were perfectly bewildered by the lands and buildings freely offered by the people, and by the hundreds of would-be enquirers desiring to be enrolled. Shop-owners offered their shops as chapels, and crowds gathered daily to hear the Gospel. Mr Montagu Beauchamp . . . was 'almost pulled to pieces by people wanting him north, south, east, and west, many days' journey off from the position in which he was located'. And Mr Beauchamp's experiences are only given as typical of others. The phrase 'as never before' became a commonplace in reports and speeches of that day—'Men crowd into our preaching halls as never before'; 'there is an eagerness for education as never before'; 'there is a friendliness towards the missionary such as there never was before.'

24

CHANGING CHINA

WILLIAM GASCOYNE-CECIL AND FLORENCE CECIL

Western views on China following the suppression of the Boxers were generally quite positive. In particular, the reforms which the Chinese undertook immediately after the Boxers impressed upon many in the West that China was a progressive country capable of change.

A case in point was a British aristocratic couple, Reverend Lord William Gascoyne-Cecil and his wife, who visited China twice in the first decade of the twentieth century. The second occasion in 1909 had the aim of researching among missionary, diplomatic, and Chinese government circles about the desirability of establishing a Western university in China. The couple came away with an extremely positive view of China. They were especially impressed with the spirit of reform throughout the country, which they called 'the new national movement'.

In the following passage they comment on the extent of change, strong enough in their minds to justify the book's title: Changing China. In the years since World War II, Western historians of this period have seen nationalism as a crucial element in the transformation taking place. The Cecils appear to concur, although they do not use the same term. But it is striking that they can also claim Christianity as one of the two main factors causing China's regeneration.

China has fundamentally altered. She used to be absolutely the most conservative land in the world. Now she is a land which is seeing so many radical changes, that a missionary said, when I asked him a question about China, 'You must not rely on me, for I left China three months ago, so that what I say may be out of date.'

China is now progressive; yes, young China believes intensely in progress, with an optimistic spirit which reminds the onlooker more of the French pre-Revolution spirit than of anything else. And this intense belief in progress shows itself at every turn; the Yamen runner has become a policeman, towns are having the benefit of water-works, schools are being opened everywhere, railways cover the land. One may well ask what has accomplished this change, what has awakened China?

Perhaps, like many other great events in history, this change of opinion in China should be attributed to more than one cause. There are two chief causes. One may be small, but it is not insignificant; the other is certainly great and obvious. The less appreciated factor that is causing the regeneration of China is Christianity; the larger and more obvious factor is the new national movement.

The Cecils also commented on the ideology of Confucianism and its relationship with ideas on government. Again their view is highly favourable and the terms in which they criticize the Chinese doctrine of 'face' appear somewhat defensive.

Confucianism does not believe in government by the people, of the people, for the people; but it believes very strongly in government for the people by the rulers. Many of its maxims might be cut out as texts, and hung up in the House of Commons with great appropriateness. It constantly pictures a well-ordered peaceful state, in which the dignity of government is well maintained, and where the working-man shall profit by his work through justice and peace, and the trader grow rich in confident security. In all this teaching it is not opposed to Western civilization. Confucius advocates the reform of society by the action of the State. Thus the sanitary laws, the education laws, the temperance laws of the West are thoroughly consistent with the teaching of Confucius. Where that teaching differs from the West is that it disbelieves in democracy. Yet Confucianism cares nothing for a man's birth: all men are born equal to the Confucianist as to the Christian; and so Confucianism has, for many centuries, welcomed people of the lowest birth as Governors, if they could pass the requisite examinations, and, having given every opportunity to men of all classes to become officials, it entrusts them and not the people with the government of the country.

In another way Confucianism is opposed to Western civilization. Confucianism believes intensely in the dignity of government; their classics are full of examples of people who, at the risk of their lives, defied kings and maintained the dignity of their positions; and this doctrine of dignity is consequently very deeply ingrained in Chinese thought; it is in reality the base of that curious doctrine of 'face' by which a man will do anything rather than confess that he is wrong. A great missionary recounts how his wonderful work at Tientsin [Tianjin] was once threatened with destruction because a boy from the south of China knocked a boy from the north off his bicycle, with the result that the college was soon divided into two factions on the question as to who should pay for the injured bicycle. The matter was only with difficulty arranged by the President paying for the bicycle and charging it to the guilty boy; but the boy did not mind paying—he minded confessing that he was wrong.

25

A LAUDATORY OBITUARY

SARAH PIKE CONGER

Much has been written about the Empress Dowager Cixi, who became Empress Dowager in 1861 and, through political moves, was able to rule China from about 1875 until her death. As seen in the extract from Broomhall, many in the West disliked her for what they perceived as her anti-foreign policies.

The Empress Dowager died on 15 November 1908, the day after her nephew, the Guangxu Emperor. Some believe there was a connection between the two deaths, and that the Empress Dowager, knowing that her last hours had come, deliberately killed her nephew so that he would not outlive her.

Notwithstanding the possibility of such an uncharitable analysis, the Empress Dowager also had her admirers. The following is the full text of the last of Sarah Pike Conger's letters from China. It is highly laudatory of the Empress Dowager, her role in China's history, and her contribution to its people, especially its women. The 'last edict' to which reference is made dictated that the Emperor's two-year-old nephew, Puyi, should ascend the throne.

November 16, 1908

The world's sympathy goes out to China this day. Official announcement is made of the death of His Imperial Majesty the Emperor of China, Kuang Hsu [Guangxu]; and of Her Imperial Majesty the Empress Dowager. Every nation has felt the touch of sorrow's hand; and now in sympathy the nations reach out to China to soothe that touch. What the nations feel I feel more keenly. The Emperor I have met many times officially. The Empress Dowager has received me, officially and socially, to an acquaintance that grew into friendship.

Her Majesty's keen perception knew the nations, and she often spoke to me with deep appreciation of America's attitude toward China. She lived a long life of usefulness, and with a steady hand, clear mind, and loyal heart, guided the affairs of her country. Through the whirlwinds of excited opinions, and through the threatening storms, this woman stood in her might and baffled them. History claims the record. This record the world recognizes; and China knows it. In my conversations with this great woman I noted her marked love for her country and for her people, and how earnestly she was reaching out to uplift the masses and to increase woman's usefulness. May this dawning of a brighter day, revealing the character of Chinese women, increase to noonday splendour; and in this splendour may the world recognize the real character of this Imperial Ruler!

For forty-seven years this able woman has stood at the head of the Chinese Empire, and strong men have given their support. In a land where woman has had so little official standing, Her Majesty's achievements make her ability and strength more pronounced; and China, surely, must be jealous for this reign in the sight of other nations. With her keen perception, this ruler recognized the future demands which were fast pressing themselves upon her people; and she worked to prepare for their wise acceptance.

Her last edict is pathetic. Weary with battlings upon the troubled sea of this life, she was ready and willing for others to stand at the helm and guide the Ship of State. 'The Dragon Throne' will in justice claim a recognition of its rights, and China's stanch men will stand loyal.

The history of her days marks the course of a strong woman's steppings. These steppings have been acknowledged by the great Chinese Empire in titles and high honors while she lived, and still greater honors after her death.

Through this woman's life the world catches a glimpse of the hidden quality of China's womanhood. It savours of a quality that might benefit that of the Western World. The Empress Dowager of China loved and honoured her great country; that country loved and honoured its great ruler. May China continue to honour her commendable deeds, and make it possible for the world to place her name among the makers of history! May China's sorrows diminish, and may her joys increase!

PART VIII

EARLY CHAOS

In 1911 the Manchu dynasty fell in a revolution which established the Republic of China. The leader of the republican revolution was Sun Yat-sen (1866–1925), who became Provisional President on 1 January 1912, but a reaction soon forced him to stand aside in favour of Yuan Shikai (1859–1916). The early years of this Republic saw chaos, with the revolutionary party ousted in the north of China and regional warlords competing for power.

In addition to the political revolution was the New Culture Movement which, from 1915, attempted to bring about social and cultural progress. Its climax was the May Fourth Movement of 1919, during which students and others demonstrated in the streets against granting Germany's interests in China to Japan, rather than to China itself. In the negotiations in Paris following the end of World War I, the powers had made just such a proposal and incorporated it into the resultant Treaty of Versailles. In political terms, the demonstrations succeeded in that China refused to sign the Treaty; the social and cultural effects continued throughout the 1920s.

Although the Boxer period represents a nadir in Western images of China, such perceptions were probably less severe in the United States than in Europe. In general, American views on China were quite supportive in the first half of the twentieth century, including the 1911 Revolution and the attempts at social progress. Moreover, the trend was upwards, so that by the time the Nationalist Party fell in 1949, the Americans felt very kindly towards China and its people. This was true of diplomats and scholars, as well as missionaries.

26
CHINESE EDUCATION
CHARLES EDMUNDS

The following extract is the introduction to Modern Education in China, *a book by Charles Edmunds, an educational missionary and President of Canton Christian College in Guangzhou. What is striking about his view, published in the same year as the May Fourth Movement, is its positive attitude towards China's modern history and attempts at modern education. Only eight years had elapsed since the fall of the Qing dynasty and less than two decades since the Boxer Uprising had produced such negative feelings about China. Yet Edmunds sees Chinese as equal to Westerners in intellectual calibre and educational experience, and even sees the Chinese as having long been democratic in spirit.*

Americans often ask: 'How do you find the Chinese students? How do they compare with American students?' My answer, after fifteen years in China, is that the distinction between the oriental and the occidental lies in technique and in knowledge, not in intellectual calibre. While there are differences in point of view and in method of approach, there is no fundamental difference in intellectual character. The Chinese conception of life's values is so different from that of western peoples that they have failed to develop modern technique and scientific knowledge. Now that they have come to see the value of these, rapid and fundamental changes are taking place. When modern scientific knowledge is added to the skill which the Chinese already have in agriculture, commerce, industry, government, and military affairs, results will be achieved which will astonish the western world.

Religion, government, and reverence for antiquity have been the dominant influences in shaping the course of Chinese education. Confucianism, Buddhism, Taoism, and for the last century

Christianity have directly and considerably influenced the development of the educational system. Unfamiliarity with the law of progress has led to undue respect for the ancient sages and has prevented radical reforms until they were imposed by the necessities of modern intercourse with the rest of the world. While the Chinese have been highly conservative, and their educational system has reflected this, their conservatism has its limits. Slow in making a departure, once the truth strikes home and its practicability is demonstrated, they do not hesitate at radical changes, nor are they discouraged by difficulties and obstructions.

The policy of providing modern education upon a national basis was adopted only a few years ago. When due allowance is made for this fact, China compares favourably in its educational history with the western world.

Though late in introducing reforms, China has always regarded education as of supreme importance. The change is not in the spirit, but in the character of the learning which that spirit admires. Formerly cherishing solely the literary and ethical excellencies of ancient Chinese classics, she now extends her admiration to the practical realities and usefulness of western science, because in them she recognizes the instruments for the realization of new national and economic ideals.

Fortunately the people of China have long been democratic in spirit and so has been their educational system. To develop the individual into a man of virtue and culture and to secure social control through raising up leaders with ability and character to influence the lives of others have been the main motives of Chinese education throughout many centuries, and may well continue even with altered content of the curricula. For China today is more in need of true men than she is of merely modern methods.

27

A LIGHT OF ORIENTAL FREEDOM

GARDNER HARDING

Gardner Harding was an American writer on China who lived there
following the 1911 Revolution. In a book with a foreword dated 17 April
1916, Harding presents himself not as a specialist, let alone an 'old China
hand', but as a supporter of revolutionary or 'Young' China. He describes
the Revolution as 'a beacon light of Oriental freedom' and himself as 'a
close friend of many of the Revolutionary leaders'. Nevertheless, he
concedes that these leaders tended to be far too given to narrow theories,
and thus unable to match such masters of political intrigue as Yuan
Shikai. Yuan defeated them, became President of the Republic, and even
briefly declared himself Emperor. Rather than having failed, Harding sees
the Revolution as merely unfinished. In his book he has 'written with
enthusiasm for Young China and with respect for Old China'.

Harding was concerned with the status and role of women. He
recognized them as being seriously oppressed under the imperial
dynasties; passages in his book refer to foot-binding and female
infanticide, and it was ills such as these that the New Culture and May
Fourth Movements sought to eradicate. In the following extract Harding
acknowledges serious deficiencies but in general puts forward an
optimistic picture of the progress women were making in 'Young China'.
He refers to Song Qingling (1892–1981) as the secretary of the leader of
the Revolution of 1911, Sun Yat-sen; Sun married Song late in 1914.

Behind these women, the leaders, the pioneers [discussed in
earlier pages], you can conceive of countless others,
dreaming, understanding, and achieving a new set of
experiences for the Chinese race. A Chinese girl can now become
a teacher or a nurse almost without restriction, and she can aspire
to be a Government student abroad, or a doctor, an editor, a civil

servant, or even a social reformer at home. The invasion of social life in general, the increasing number of women's papers, not all of which have been snuffed out in the reaction, the vast increase of girl students, and the profoundly changing relation of women to the home, are all deeply significant.

One should never lose sight, however, of the characteristic Chinese strain which makes this movement like nothing else in the world.

The invasion in social life most noticeable in Japan, for instance, is the flood of girls who in recent years have entered the world of business. In China this phenomenon is completely absent, and shows no signs of developing for years to come. Miss C. R. Soong [Song Qingling], Dr Sun's charming secretary, claimed to be the only woman in China who worked in a man's office, and unless other cases of purely 'patriotic' employment furnish like exceptions, her claim was literally true. There are no Chinese typists, no Chinese shopgirls, no Chinese ticket takers, not any women at all, except Eurasian and foreign girls, in the endless business employments that they occupy in the Western and the Japanese worlds. The up-to-date YWCA [Young Women's Christian Association] trains many capable stenographers and typists; but for employment under women only, as in mission schools, hospitals, and purely private office work. This taboo against women's employment is even supported by Young China; for the revolution is primarily one of mind, and the new opportunities it stresses for women are distinctly mental opportunities.

A more material revolution, however, has introduced Chinese women of the lowest classes to factory labour. The cotton mills of Shanghai alone employ 25,000 women and young girls twelve hours day and night, with a sixteen-hour day on Saturdays, for wages that average twelve to fifteen cents a day. The middle classes can enforce their boycott on the business world, but modern industry is catching the women of the poor in the gigantic net of economic evolution. Factories run by woman and child labour pay 57 per cent annual profit in Shanghai, and by that door Western industrialism is entering more rapidly every year into the lives of the women of China. As yet there are no laws, either against the foreigner, who is mainly responsible for these things, or for the Chinese, who are so far merely their minor competitors. There are no laws, no statistics, and hardly any general knowledge or consideration.

Now in this stratum of the national life, now in that, the pervasive hand of evolution ceaselessly continues in its enduring work of alteration in the status of women. This revolution has been no mere ephemeral effervescence of the coast cities; it has penetrated to the ultimate hearthstone of the people on whom all Chinese civilization rests—the countless millions of the peasantry. It has reached them because it possesses the only quality in the world that could reach them: it is above all a moral revolution. Consider the three great reforms in Chinese home life that have accompanied it—the crusades against the opium traffic, against foot binding, and against child slavery; one charter of freedom each for the man, the woman, and the child, but all three supremely the concern of women as keepers and conservers of the home. How terribly far from completion all these reforms are only those know who have seen the degradation and compelling poverty at first hand of the life of the mass of the Chinese people. But this much is certain: that the spirit of these reforms and the quality of mind of the Revolution, have got home to the common people in a way, be it ever so little, that will inevitably tend steadily to raise the lot of women in years to come. They have created something more nearly like a national renaissance in the moral fibre of the people than any other period of social reform recorded about China.

Like the woman [sic] movement all over the world, the emergence of women in China is above everything a spirit of humanism, a regeneration of enduring instincts for good in both sexes, and a widening of that area of contact and understanding between men and women which inexorably grows with civilization. In their capacity for progress there are, I believe, no women in Asia like the women of China. Beside Japan, China is counted as one of the world's weak nations. But in the moral regeneration that is bringing about the emergence into modern life of her woman she is fulfilling a deeper and more authentic test of civilization than has been met by Japan in all her fifty headlong years of material progress.

28

A MARTYRED SOUL

W. Somerset Maugham (1874–1965) was among the giants of British literature of his time. Most of his 'Asian' stories are set in Borneo, Malaya, or Singapore, but his play East of Suez *premiered in 1922, and about half his novel* The Painted Veil*, first published in 1925, is set in China. Maugham travelled in China for about four months in 1919 and 1920, and wrote a travel book of his impressions, entitled* On a Chinese Screen*, which was published in 1922. This is full of the warm, personal style characteristic of its author, with many subjective but penetrating observations on what he saw, heard, and smelt and, above all, to the people he met. Although designed as reality, it reads a bit like the fiction of which Maugham was such a master.*

The following extract concerns a missionary, Mr Wingrove, with whom Maugham stayed briefly during his China visit, the mission being just outside a populous city. Mr Wingrove was English, like most of the people who interested Maugham, but had not been home for seventeen years. Although he had a substantial library he told Maugham that he read but rarely. According to Maugham, Wingrove's wife 'was not a lady. She had a vulgar intonation'. In the following passage Maugham interprets how he believed Mr Wingrove felt towards the Chinese, with passing observations on his wife's views. Characteristically for Maugham, just a brief succession of facial expressions is enough to set off an analysis of what is going on in somebody's mind. The chapter from which the extract is drawn is entitled 'Fear'.

There was something odd about the man. At last, as was inevitable, I suppose, he began to talk of the Chinese. Mrs Wingrove said the same things about them that I had already heard so many missionaries say. They were a lying people, untrustworthy, cruel, and dirty, but a faint light was visible in the East; though the results of missionary endeavour were not very noteworthy as yet, the future was promising. They no longer believed in their old gods and the power of the literati was broken. It is an attitude of mistrust and dislike tempered by optimism. But Mr Wingrove mitigated his wife's strictures. He dwelt on the good-nature of the Chinese, on their devotion to their parents and on their love for their children.

'Mr Wingrove won't hear a word against the Chinese,' said his wife, 'he simply loves them.'

'I think they have great qualities,' he said. 'You can't walk through those crowded streets of theirs without having that impressed on you.'

'I don't believe Mr Wingrove notices the smells,' his wife laughed.

At that moment there was a knock at the door and a young woman came in. She had the long skirts and the unbound feet of the native Christian, and on her face a look that was at once cringing and sullen. She said something to Mrs Wingrove. I happened to catch sight of Mr Wingrove's face. When he saw her, there passed over it an expression of the most intense physical repulsion, it was distorted as though by an odour that nauseated him, and then immediately it vanished and his lips twitched to a pleasant smile; but the effort was too great and he showed only a tortured grimace. I looked at him with amazement. Mrs Wingrove with an 'excuse me' got up and left the room.

'That is one of our teachers,' said Mr Wingrove in that same set voice which had a little puzzled me before. 'She's invaluable. I put infinite reliance on her. She has a very fine character.'

Then, I hardly know why, in a flash I saw the truth; I saw the disgust in his soul for all that his will loved. I was filled with the excitement which an explorer may feel when after a hazardous journey he comes upon a country with features new and unexpected. Those tortured eyes explained themselves, the unnatural voice, the measured restraint with which he praised, that air he had of a hunted man. Notwithstanding all he said he hated the Chinese with a hatred beside which his wife's distaste was insignificant. When he walked through the teeming streets of the city it was an agony to him, his missionary life revolted him, his soul was like the raw shoulders of the coolies and the carrying pole burnt the bleeding wound. He would not go home because he could not bear to see again what he cared for so much, he would not read his books because they reminded him of the life he loved so passionately, and perhaps he had married that vulgar wife in order to cut himself off more resolutely from a world that his every instinct craved for. He martyred his tortured soul with a passionate exasperation.

29

PLENTY WRONG WITH CHINA

RODNEY GILBERT

In the early to mid-1920s China continued to be deeply divided. Warlords persisted in fighting for power. In the south the nationalist leader Sun Yat-sen and his successor Chiang Kai-shek ran a government based in Guangzhou, but it, too, had to fend off attacks from local warlords. In 1926, the year after Sun's death, Chiang Kai-shek began his Northern Expedition in an attempt to reunify the country.

In the mid-1920s several books appeared in the West attacking China and the Chinese, of which the most famous was Rodney Gilbert's What's Wrong with China, *published in 1926. Writers like the Chinese philosopher Lin Yutang thought Gilbert's view typical of the West. The Chinese government, according to Gilbert, was already fostering a fiercely anti-foreign line, taken up enthusiastically by the people. What writers like Gilbert wanted was for the Western powers to intervene militarily to sort out China's problems, since China was obviously incapable of doing so itself.*

Ironically, Gilbert claims to like the Chinese. If he were to write 'all that he likes, admires, and loves in China and the Chinese, he would produce, in due course of years, a book as monstrously huge as some of China's own reference works'. Yet the tone of his book is both condescending and racist.

An unbiased observer, going to and fro in the world, must observe that breeds of men differ, almost as widely as individuals, in temperament and capacity as well as in physical appearance, language, customs, and culture. There are inferior races in the world, just as there are inferior men in every community. There are nations that cannot government themselves, but must have a master, just as there are men in every community that need a guardian and are a menace to the community if granted the unqualified 'right to life, liberty, and the pursuit of happiness'. Races, like men, have their limitations. Education and environment, law and the exercise of it, may make the inferior man a more useful and less dangerous member of the community, but he is born with certain distinct limitations beyond which no amount of education or training can carry him. When such a man is told by kind sentimentalists that he is as good as any other and is entitled to as much, he blames society for his failures, and bitterly resents the success of others. There is no hatred like that of the conscious inferior for the superior. . . .

Old residents in China who have for many years been perplexed by the strange and erratic reactions of the Chinese and have been almost ready to admit that there was some baffling element in their mental make-up, which vexed them as much as an organic impurity does the analytical chemist when he thinks he is dealing with simple inorganic compounds, have suddenly found, when they had children of their own to study and understand, that the difference between the Eastern and Western mentality is precisely the same as the difference between the puerile and adult mind; that the famous barrier between East and West is like nothing so much as the barrier of adolescence that stands between the sympathies of ten and twenty.

To the adult who has forgotten his childhood, as so many have, the Chinese and the child are each a bundle of likeable, amusing but perplexing and often irritating contradictions.

The Chinese have all the native charm of children and all their weaknesses. They are kind, as children are kind; and cruel, as children are cruel. Children either love a pet to death or subject it to tortures that would shame the lowest savage just to see it squirm and squeal—so do the Chinese indulge themselves. Highly cultured Chinese officials, who are so high-strung that they shudder at the suggestion of pain, can watch a man being skinned alive with an eager interest that becomes no one but a child. The Chinese are as trustful and loyal as children, and yet suspicious, secretive, and circuitous in their methods as only children can be. They are suspicious and sensitive, but affectionate and trusting—as only children are. Like children they are wilful, proud, independent, recalcitrant, and resentful of correction, but under sustained and reasonable discipline are the most docile, tractable, and responsive people on earth—like nothing so much in fact as good schoolboys. We all know how graspingly mean and selfish a child can be at one moment and how foolishly and lavishly generous he can be the next, acting under impulses which we cannot grasp; the Chinese are the same. They are timid, but bold; peace loving, but warlike; painstaking and indefatigable workers, and at the same time careless, slipshod, and shirking, just as they happen to be used and inspired, as children are.

The Chinese love cliques, as children do. They display a high power of organization in guilds, secret societies, conferences, and meetings of all sorts, *under authority*. . . . Finally, like children and animals, they squirm under ridicule, find everything most amusing but themselves, and simply abhor the person who refuses to take them seriously.

Superficially China has a great many serious problems to face and the world has much to do to arrange for lasting placid relations between the East and West. But it is the purpose of these essays to demonstrate what will here be stated as a fundamental hypothesis: that most of China's ills have grown out of her own and our failure to appreciate that the Chinese mind is a child's mind—the mind of a precocious child at its best and worst. If China's ills are to be laid at our door, as her propagandists say, it is because we have failed to realize that we are dealing with children, because we have treated the individual Chinese as an adult and the nation as a grown-up.

Books such as these provoked reaction. One, which frequently quotes and directly attacks Gilbert's book, is O. D. Rasmussen's What's Right with China, *which was published in 1928 by the Commercial Press in Shanghai. The book is extremely friendly towards China and to the revolution taking place at the time. It is dedicated to the young men and women of China whose exalted idealism is leading their country from the stagnant marshes of an alien-imposed regression to the hard highway of progress.*

Rasmussen, a Dane, is certainly worth mentioning because he, like some other Westerners, was prepared to attack Rodney Gilbert and his ilk and defend China. (No extract given.)

30

A BLEAK VIEW

A. F. LEGENDRE

TRANSLATED BY ELSIE MARTIN JONES

France also produced racist observers fiercely critical of China. One such was A. F. Legendre, who lived most of the first quarter of the twentieth century in China, mainly in Sichuan Province, travelling extensively in Yunnan, Shanxi, Sichuan, and elsewhere. Legendre believed that 'the functioning powers of the different organs in the yellow man are inferior to those of the white'. In his view the Chinese suffered from a 'physical decadence consequent on torpor of the nerves in a people unaccustomed to, if not incapable of, effort, whose benumbed brain is awakened only by violent sensations.' He believed that the Western powers should intervene to save China from the political chaos, 'an evolution backwards' into which it had fallen since the overthrow of the Manchus in 1911.

Legendre describes China as a once 'great country' with a splendid ancient wisdom that has fallen into disrepair and anarchy. He is particularly scathing about two major features of traditional China, the literati class and the family system, the first being totally corrupt and self-serving, the second abominably cruel, especially towards women. But he also sees the family system as the anchor which held Chinese society together but made the Chinese incapable of acting as a united people.

In the following extract from his book Modern Chinese Civilization, *Legendre sums up his view of Chinese politics, society, economy, and health since the 1911 Revolution.*

I n China there has never been any political unity, any more than ethnic or social unity.

Never has a country seen more revolutions and civil wars; and if it has survived, it can be said that it owes its life to its great distance from Europe.

Save for short periods of their history, the different provinces of China have lived a self-governing life under the control, more nominal than real, of Pekin [Beijing], and have remained indifferent to each other's fate, even in time of war.

The Viceroys, as also the high mandarins, are only tax collectors. The notables of every village, canton, or city, carry on the administration on their own responsibility, and themselves maintain the roads and canals of their district.

Thus, where there is no collective effort, there is no community of soul or sentiment. The general interest is ignored. The mandarin who has paid for his right to enrich himself is never sure of the morrow. He is then in a hurry to heap up money for his old age, and is concerned with himself and not with his district. Thus it is from top to bottom of the mandarin ladder.

When we therefore examine the élite, the privileged class of *literati* of whom Confucius is the prototype, we cannot help holding this class responsible in great part for the past and present situation of China. It lived in isolation from the masses, set up on a pedestal, admiring itself and glorifying itself with an unfathomable pride.

The system of education and instruction which it had created ceased to stimulate its intelligence, or give it any creative energy. Thus it became stereotyped in the acquisitions of the past— acquisitions whose source must be looked for in Western Asia.

On the other hand, ignoring the maxim *mens sana in corpore sano*, this class lived all the time in absolute bodily idleness, avoiding all movement and effort, going about only in a palanquin, and never using its muscles—disdainful also of open spaces and that marvellous health-giver, fresh air—but on the contrary greedy of the joys of the table and the harem.

In the practical sphere, the mandarin, always a member of the too bookish lettered class, and contemptuous of all besides his classics, has been a wretched ruler; large ideas are foreign to him. He has never been able either to muster or to co-ordinate what is at his disposal, nor subsequently known how to frame a constructive policy when it is a question of the needs of the country as against the sum of its resources. There has never been a general budget for the empire, a budget worthy of the name.

When, on the other hand, you consider the great economic organizations of China—railways, ports, factories, mining operations—you are forced to realize that without European help the Chinese would achieve only a mediocre return or even a rapid diminution of these industries. The railroads that he is now working, so prosperous in the days of European management, are to-day in a lamentable state, neither permanent way nor rolling stock being maintained.

Has the Chinaman at least been able to defend himself against the periodic scourges which have regularly assailed him during long centuries—against flood, for instance, or against epidemics? No; he is still totally powerless in face of them; he is devoured by tuberculosis and syphilis; and cholera, the plague, smallpox, and typhus fever take toll of him to an extent no European can imagine.

He is so immensely ignorant of hygiene that he is the victim of all the possible contagions, and he has remained in the age of lice and vermin, while the victims of itch and scab are innumerable.

As, on the other hand, infantile mortality exceeds 50 per cent, it is vain and absurd to go on speaking of 400 millions of Chinese. My statistics allow me to affirm that there are at most 300 millions, and that the population is not increasing.

One circumstance, however, one religion has saved China, and has preserved her through the ages from extinction: and that is

A Chinese family wiped out, photograph taken on the way from Shanghai to Wusong, late 1920s. Photograph by Arthur Hodges. Courtesy of Joscelyn Burn.

British forces on patrol in Shanghai, 1925. Photograph by Arthur Hodges.
Courtesy of Joscelyn Burn.

ancestral worship, involving the dogma of procreation to the utmost extent, under penalty of every calamity for the disobedient.

It is this China, however, nearer the Middle Ages than the twentieth century, which in 1911 determined to pass abruptly from her secular absolutism to a democratic system.

You know what this experience has cost her during fifteen years—poverty in the midst of anarchy, an immense poignant distress, and the loss of twenty millions of her population by civil war and famine.

This is the balance sheet of the Chinese republic from 1911 to this day, the balance sheet of a period of veritable retrogression, comparable only to the Bolshevist experiment.

PART IX

THE NANJING DECADE

*I*n 1927 Chiang Kai-shek and his Nationalist Party, the Kuomintang (Guomindang), succeeded in establishing a regime which proved more stable than any since the fall of the Manchu dynasty. With its capital in Nanjing from 1927 to 1937 and again after World War II, this regime is often described as 'the Nanjing government' and its first ten years as 'the Nanjing decade'. In 1928 Chiang completed the Northern Expedition and at the end of the year the Manchurian warlord Zhang Xueliang submitted to Chiang, thus signalling China's formal reunification. Yet Chiang continued to face enormous opposition internally and the Japanese, who had already sent troops to parts of the country, actually set up a puppet state covering the whole of Manchuria in China's north-east in 1932. Japan continued to encroach on China during the following years, leading to all-out war from the middle of 1937.

31

POOR CHINA!

ARNOLD TOYNBEE

A famous visitor to China in the early part of Chiang Kai-shek's rule was the British historian Arnold Toynbee (1889–1975), remembered chiefly for his A Study of History. *He worked on this mammoth achievement virtually his whole life from 1921 onward; Oxford University Press published it in twelve volumes from 1934 to 1961 and in a single abridged version in 1972. In this work, enormous in scope and scale, Toynbee advanced a general historical theory concerning the rise and decline of civilizations.*

At the end of 1929 and the beginning of 1930 Toynbee made a short trip to Manchuria, Beijing, Nanjing, and other parts of China as part of six months' travel around the Old World from July 1929 to the end of January 1930. His erudition and eye for detail are obvious in his comments about China. Toynbee's observations are very positive about China's people and civilization, and he is particularly enthusiastic about Beijing, because of its 'marvellous symmetry' and because, unlike other great cities such as Constantinople (Istanbul), Rome, and New York, it did not depend at all on nature for its awe-inspiring magnificence.

In the following passage Toynbee turns his hand to the present and to politics, about which he is considerably less positive. He extrapolates from conversations with people he met to judge the Kuomintang and the situation in China in the late 1920s. The extract illustrates his willingness to make sweeping generalizations, which irritated many people, including fellow historians. Yet Toynbee never fails to interest, even when talking about matters which he does not pretend to understand in depth.

U nder kind and distinguished and most efficient auspices, I was enabled during my brief stay in Nanking [Nanjing] to meet the most prominent personalities in the present

Government of the Chinese Republic. It was an interesting moment for making acquaintance with them; for in those closing days of December 1929, the Kuomintang Government had just emerged from an internal storm in which they had almost foundered; . . . In these circumstances I had the opportunity to admire the cool-headedness and restrained vitality of General Chiang Kai-shek and the intellectual driving power and workmanlike modesty of Mr T.V. Soong [Song Ziwen], the Minister of Finance. But it would be unsuitable to requite the courtesy with which I was received at Nanking by enlarging upon my very superficial impressions of these gentlemen's characters and attainments. I will only say that I came away with a high opinion of certain individuals in high places. As for my opinion of the Kuomintang Party—the authority in whose name these individuals exercise their power—about that I am not so sure.

My opinion of the Kuomintang Party (for whatever that opinion may be worth) is mainly based on a conversation which I had at Nanking with a prominent Party member, a man who has taken an active part in the movement from early days and who prefers to make himself felt in Party committees rather than in offices of State. There was something attractive about him—attractive and at the same time exasperating, for, under the mask of a grown man's face, there seemed to be peeping out at me the countenance of an irresponsible and impish boy, and I felt that here I was in the presence of something very characteristic of the Kuomintang; characteristic, indeed, of all Chinese politics and perhaps of all Chinese life—at least, since China has been trying to rejuvenate herself by grafts from the monkey-glands of Western culture.

I had come to Nanking with a strong sense that all the Chinese whom I had been meeting elsewhere, and who were not professional politicians, were profoundly discouraged by the recrudescence of civil war and disunity in 1929 after the apparent achievement of unity and peace in 1928. Their strictures upon the politicians had been openly contemptuous, and I had begun to wonder how much longer the politicians would have licence to pursue their Party and personal ends at the people's cost. The catchword of 'Unity', it seemed to me, had lost all its glamour; the one passionate desire of the Chinese people was for peace, and if the politicians ventured to sacrifice the reality of peace to the will-o'-the-wisp of unity again, I fancied that they might have short

A Chinese woman being executed for killing her husband, early 1930s.
Photograph by Arthur Hodges. Courtesy of Joscelyn Burn.

shrift this time. With this picture sharply stamped on my mind, I entered into conversation with my Party man at Nanking, and in the course of our talk about the political situation of the moment I threw out the suggestion that, in the competition between rival Governments and parties and war-lords in China, the ultimate victory would fall not to those who sought to impose unity by force but to those who sought to give the people the things that the people wanted deep down in their hearts. 'You are quite right,' said the Party man, brightly. 'We certainly ought to learn how to use the people. If we don't, we shall find our opponents using them against us.' Use the people! This too sorely tried, too tamely long-suffering people, whose miseries touch the heart even of the casual passing foreign traveller! And that was how they were regarded by one of their own countrymen who was supposed to be a shepherd of the people during the 'period of tutelage' of Dr Sun Yat-sen's political apocalypse! And he had spoken it out so naïvely, without the ghost of a notion of how deeply he was shocking me! (Had he suspected, he would certainly have checked his utterance, for he was an adroit politician, and evidently wanted me to carry away a good impression of the Party and of himself as its representative.) Poor China!

And yet I did find one true shepherd of the people in Nanking—not in high places, nor, indeed, in politics at all, but in the Extension Service of the Department of Agriculture of the University. He too was a man of ability. For instance, he spoke

English fluently, though he had never visited an English-speaking country and it had never been particularly his business to pick the language up. I fancy he could have been in politics and been successful in them—if he had wished; but, no, he had chosen a different career. His mission was to travel round the villages, teaching the peasants how to improve their methods of agriculture and teaching them other things as well: not to bind their daughters' feet, and not to sell their tiny patrimonies (those two or three mow [*mu*; unit of land] which in China make all the difference between a peasant proprietor and a landless pauper) in order to make the traditional display at marriages and funerals. The work was arduous and slow and often disheartening. 'If one is educated,' he burst out, for an instant departing from his reserve— 'if one is educated to a liberal understanding of the use and meaning of life, it cuts one to the heart to see the poor peasants fast bound in the misery and iron of these misguided customs.' That man has a heart, and it is he and his like who, quite unknown to fame, are carrying the burdens of China on their shoulders.

32

AN APPLE A DAY

CARL CROW

One of the substantial group of long-term foreign residents in China in the interwar years was Carl Crow. He represents not only the 'old China hand', a familiar breed, but also a category much less familiar in these pages so far, namely the 'advertising and merchandising agent', as he calls himself. This job led him to live in China for about a quarter of a century, leaving only with the outbreak of war against Japan in 1937. His book Four Hundred Million Customers *has a most appropriate title, telling the reader the basic avowed aim of all his activities in China: he wanted to profit from the country.*

Despite, or perhaps because of, such an intention, Crow was a man of goodwill towards China and liked the Chinese. He ends the preface of his book by explaining that he wishes to give the reader 'a new understanding of the interesting, exasperating, puzzling, and, almost always, lovable Chinese people as I have known them'.

In the following passage, Crow discusses the progress he sees towards selling to the Chinese. The chapter from which it is taken, 'An Apple a Day', discusses the opportunities of sales involved in the simple proposition that an apple a day would keep the doctor away in China just as elsewhere. In this passage, he is specifically talking about all Chinese men, not just the rich. The example of cigarettes to show good salesmanship was perfectly appropriate in the 1930s.

Despite his occasional light-heartedness, Crow had strong feelings about the country which was his home for so long; no reader of his book I Speak for the Chinese *can be left in any doubt about that. This book is a study of Sino-Japanese relations from 1915 to 1937 and a passionate indictment of Japanese policy and behaviour.*

Since the beginning of the present century, China's purchases of foreign goods have shown a constantly changing picture of the wants of the Chinese people. In 1900 the total sale of cigarettes in China was 200 million, or less than one per person per annum. Ten years later it had jumped to 7,500 million or, say, about 19 per annum. In another ten years it was 22,000 million or 60 per annum. Now it amounts to 80,000 million or, practically a daily cigarette for every male resident of the country. In the meantime, the sale of imported cotton goods has dropped from more than 50 per cent of the total to less than 3 per cent. Importations of 'candles, soaps, oils, fats, waxes, gums, and resins' now amount to more than importations of cotton cloth. This does not mean a decrease in the demand for cotton goods, but the development of a new source of supply. Most of the cotton goods they now buy are produced in local mills owned by Japanese, Chinese, and British.

The Chinese were a long time making up their minds that they wanted any of the modern articles manufactured by the West, but once they started buying they found that they wanted everything they could afford to buy and a good deal more. Now they are buying aeroplanes, motor-cars, and, among other modern things, laundry machinery. The catalogue of China's wants is no longer restricted by ignorance and prejudice, but solely by ability to purchase. In fact, China's 400 million customers face the same problem as that which confronts the lady who has a shopping list which calls for an expenditure of [US]$10 and has only $4.95 in her purse. Before anything is purchased, it is necessary to give

Japanese occupation troops in Shanghai during the 1930s. Photograph by Arthur Hodges. Courtesy of Joscelyn Burn.

Entitled 'Chinese Wives Have Much More Leisure', this picture implies that Crow
is talking more about women of the better-off classes, those in families rich
enough to employ servants and dress well. Source: Carl Crow, drawings by G.
Sapojnikoff, *Four Hundred Million Customers.*

careful consideration to the value and desirability of that article in
comparison with similar articles, and also in comparison with a
number of other articles of an entirely different nature. This is true
of small as well as large purchases and is strikingly illustrated by the
annual summer slump in the cigarette business. The many varieties
of melons which come on the market in June provide about the
only uncooked food the Chinese eat and there is a universal
demand for them, but many cannot afford the twin luxuries of
melons and cigarettes. As a result, some give up cigarettes for
melons, and cigarette consumption does not resume normal
proportions until the melon season is over, in the early autumn.

Thus, every sale that is made in China is the result of successful
competition not only with similar articles made by a competitor,
but with a wide variety of other things with which it would not
appear to have any particular connection. The apple eater, for
example, would, like the melon eater, have to choose between fruit
and cigarettes and then, if the choice fell on fruit, apples would
have to run the gamut of all other fruits before a sale was made.
This introduces into the selling of goods to China complications
which are measured by the geometric rather than the arithmetical
progression, and adds grey hairs to the heads of sales managers
and advertising agents.

33

CHINESE PEASANTS

PEARL BUCK

A remarkable observer of China in the first half of the twentieth century
was Pearl Buck (1892–1973). A writer, mainly of fiction, she was born in
the United States, the daughter of Presbyterian missionaries. When she
was only three months old, her parents took her to China, where she lived
until the mid-1930s, coming to regard it as home.

By far her most famous work is the novel The Good Earth, *published in*
New York in 1931, which proved so successful that it sold over four million
copies during her lifetime. Its main character is a Chinese peasant whose
concerns are land and position, and she treats his life and that of his slave-
wife with the utmost sympathy. This novel contributed more than any
other single work to a positive view of China in the West, particularly in the
United States. Being a novel, it lies outside the scope of this book. However,
Buck wrote an autobiography in which she comments on the Chinese
peasants and describes writing the novel. Considering the novel's success,
it is worth mentioning that she was uncertain of its value, but decided to
try to get it published anyway: 'I tied up the pages and mailed them off to
New York myself, and prepared to wait while I busied myself with other
work'.

At this period of my life and of China's history I was keenly
aware of the Chinese peasant, his wonderful strength and
goodness, his amusing and often alarming shrewdness
and wisdom, his cynicism and his simplicity, his direct approach to
life which is the habit of a deep and natural sophistication. It
seemed to me that the Chinese peasant, who comprised 85 per
cent of China's population, was so superior a human group, that it
was a loss to humanity that he was also voiceless because he was

illiterate. And it was this group, so charming, so virile, so genuinely civilized in spite of illiteracy and certain primitive conditions of life that might very well be merely the result of enforced mental isolation from the currents of modern thinking and discovery, whom the young moderns, rootless and ruthless, proposed to 'educate.' Nothing in Communist theory enrages me more than Trotsky's callous remark that the peasants are the 'packhorses' of a nation. Who made them packhorses? And to what heights may not these 'packhorses' rise if they are considered human beings instead of beasts of burden? For in all my years in China I never ceased to feel intolerable pain and anger when I looked into the thin intelligent face of some Chinese peasant twisted into sheer physical agony because on his back he bore a burden too much even for a beast. I have seen his slender legs quiver under the weight of a two-hundred-pound bag of rice, or under the huge wardrobe trunk of some travelling foreign tourist. Edwin Markham's poem 'The Man with the Hoe,' discovered late by me, gave me a wonderful catharsis of the spirit. Here was an American who could have understood the whole problem of Asia. And my continuing regret concerning Asian leaders is that so few of them have understood the quality of their own peasants, and therefore few have valued this mighty and common man of the earth.

And among them the Communists are the most guilty, for with all their talk, I do not see that they have valued this man, either,

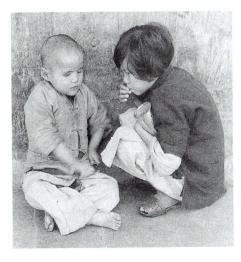

Two beggar children in the 1930s. Photograph by Arthur Hodges. Courtesy of Joscelyn Burn.

A shop street scene in Shanghai, 1930s. Photograph by Arthur Hodges. Courtesy of Joscelyn Burn.

and their condescension to him makes my soul sick. Yesterday in New York a young Chinese women sat in my small living room and told me breathlessly of the great and marvellous changes that the Communists are making in China. And in her words, too, I caught the old stink of condescension.

34

COMRADES

AGNES SMEDLEY

The Chinese Communist Party (CCP) was set up in 1921 in the wake of the New Culture Movement, but was defeated utterly in 1927 by the forces of Chiang Kai-shek. Instead of giving up, the CCP went to the countryside and in November 1931 its leader, Mao Zedong, was able to set up the Chinese Soviet Republic in Jiangxi Province, with its capital in Ruijin. Chiang Kai-shek led five military campaigns against this Soviet Republic, the last of which succeeded in destroying it late in 1934.

Few people in the West took serious notice of the Soviet Republic, and even fewer supported it. One who admired it very strongly, however, was the American radical socialist and feminist journalist Agnes Smedley (1892–1950). Born of a poor background, she early became involved in the international socialist movement, going to the Soviet Union and then to China in 1928. In the following passage she sums up the regimes led by Chiang Kai-shek in Nanjing and Mao Zedong in Ruijin, describing how each reacted to the Japanese.

The Chinese Soviets and their defender, the Chinese Red Army, have developed against a background of official Kuomintang China in which wild counter-revolution has raged, preparing the way for the inevitable armed foreign intervention which today threatens completely to dismember China. The Nanking [Nanjing] Government, officially recognized by foreign powers as 'the' Chinese Government, has taken not one sincere or serious step to halt the dismemberment and subjection of the country. On the contrary, it has signed a series of treaties with the imperial Japanese Government delivering many Chinese Provinces to Japanese rule. . . .

In January of 1934 the second All-Chinese Congress of Soviets met in Shuikin [Ruijin], the Soviet capital, and Mau Tse-tung [Mao Zedong], President of the Chinese Soviet Republic, reviewed conditions and changes within the Soviet regions since the first Congress in November 1931.

The revolutionary progress made in the Chinese Soviet regions is the explanation for the new successes of the Chinese Red Army. The anti-feudal, agrarian land revolution has been carried to completion. A sound economic and financial policy has consolidated Soviet power and won the most passionate support of the masses within the Soviet regions and even in the Kuomintang areas beyond whose populations are bent under the fearful burdens of feudal and capitalist exploitation. The laws passed at the first Congress of the Soviet have been put into effect and drastically improved the conditions of all workers and peasants.

Great cultural progress has likewise taken place. Thousands of schools, night schools, clubs, and classes for the eradication of illiteracy have been founded. There are many normal schools and other institutions for the training of women, and a central University at Shuikin has two thousand men and women under training. Newspapers, wall newspapers, exhibitions, revolutionary theatrical groups, have added their share to a new cultural life. The central Military Academy of the Red Army near Shuikin has graduated two classes of commanders in 1933 alone, each class numbering 1,500.

The Red Army has become an iron army of the Chinese Revolution. The formation of the Central Revolutionary Military Council of the Soviet Government at the end of 1931 has enabled all the Red Armies to fight and operate in coordination and under unified tactics. The Council established more intimate contacts with all other armed organizations of the people, such as Partisans, Red Guards, Young Vanguards, militiamen; and the unarmed mass organizations, such as contact squads, transport, reconnoitering, medical aid, hygiene, divisional detachments—all of which take a direct part in military work at the front and in the rear.

For the inevitable war to free China from foreign imperialist control the Chinese Soviet Government issued a call in 1932 for a Red Army of a million men. The response has been very great. From Kuomintang-imperialist cities thousands of industrial workers have gone into the Soviet regions to join the Red Army.

A Chinese family in the 1930s. Photograph by Arthur Hodges. Courtesy of
Joscelyn Burn.

New model shock divisions and corps consisting of industrial workers and handworkers from the Soviet regions have been also organized. Some shock divisions are composed entirely of Communists or Young Communists; others have at times as high as 60 or 70 per cent Communists.

Despite these achievements, the Chinese Soviet Republic was defeated by Chiang Kai-shek's troops in October 1934. Just as in 1927, the CCP refused to give up, instead undertaking its epic Long March. After a year of hardships, this extraordinary achievement took the CCP and the Red Army to the other end of the country, northern Shaanxi, where they established their headquarters in Yan'an.

35
LITTLE RED DEVILS

EDGAR SNOW

Possibly the most remarkable of all Western observers of the Chinese Communist Party in the 1930s was the American journalist Edgar Snow (1905–72), from Missouri. In 1936 he had the unique opportunity to visit the CCP's northern Shaanxi revolutionary base. Not only did he interview Mao Zedong, but he recorded impressions and experiences in great detail. The result was the classic work Red Star Over China, *first published in London by Victor Gollancz in 1937 and the next year by Random House in New York. It quickly became a best-seller among the left in Britain, although Snow's own country was more reserved in its acceptance of the book.*

Snow's impressions from his visit were remarkably positive. While this made both the book and its author controversial in the West, both were lionized in China itself when the CCP came to power. Snow made several return visits during the period when Mao Zedong was in control.

In the following passage from the chapter entitled 'Little Red Devils', Snow discusses the Communist Youth League's organization of boys and very young men, called Young Vanguards, which the League's secretary claimed to have a membership of some 40,000 in the north-west soviet districts. His comments show both his positive attitude to the Communists and his sense of humour.

I met a youth of fourteen who had been an apprentice in a Shanghai machine shop, and with three companions had found his way, through various adventures, to the Northwest. He was a student in the radio school in Pao An [Bao'an, northern Shaanxi] when I saw him. I asked whether he missed Shanghai, but he said no, he had left nothing in Shanghai, and that the only fun

135

he had ever had there was looking into the shop windows at good things to eat—which he could not buy.

One 'little devil' in Pao An served as orderly to Li K'e-nung [Li Kenong], chief of the communications department of the Foreign Office. He was a Shansi [Shanxi province] lad of about thirteen or fourteen, and he had joined the Reds I knew not how. The Beau Brummell of the Vanguards, he took his role with utmost gravity. He had inherited a Sam Browne belt from somebody, he had a neat little uniform tailored to a good fit, and a cap whose peak he regularly refilled with new cardboard whenever it broke. Underneath the collar of his well-brushed coat he always managed to have a strip of white linen showing. He was easily the snappiest-looking soldier in town. Beside him Mao Tse-tung [Zedong] looked a tramp.

This *wa-wa's* [child's] name happened by some thoughtlessness of his parents to be Shang Chi-pang [Jibang]. There is nothing wrong with that, except that Chi-pang sounds very much like *chi-pa*, and so, to his unending mortification, he was often called *chi-pa*, which simply means 'penis.' One day Chi-pang came into my little room in the Foreign Office with his usual quota of dignity, clicked his heels together, gave me the most Prussian-like salute I had seen in the Red districts, and addressed me as 'Comrade Snow'. He then proceeded to unburden his small heart of certain apprehensions. What he wanted to do was to make it perfectly clear to me that his name was

 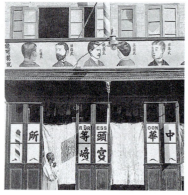

Shop signs in Shanghai photographed by a British resident during the 1930s, giving some idea of what interested British residents during the period. Photograph by Arthur Hodges. Courtesy of Joscelyn Burn.

not Chi-pa, but Chi-pang, and that between these two there was all the difference in the world. He had his name carefully scrawled down on a scrap of paper, and this he deposited before me.

Astonished, I responded in all seriousness that I had never called him anything but Chi-pang, and had no thought of doing otherwise. He thanked me, made a grave bow, and once more gave that preposterous salute. 'I wanted to be sure,' he said, 'that when you write about me for the foreign papers you won't make a mistake in my name. It would give a bad impression to the foreign comrades if they thought a Red soldier was named Chi-pa!' Until then I had had no intention of introducing Chi-pang into this strange book, but with that remark I had no choice in the matter, and he walked into it right beside the Generalissimo. . . .

Altogether, the 'little devils' were one thing in Red China with which is was hard to find anything seriously wrong. Their spirit was superb. I suspected that more than once an older man, looking at them, forgot his pessimism and was heartened to think that he was fighting for the future of lads like those. They were invariably cheerful and optimistic, and they had a ready '*hao!*' [good] for every how-are-you, regardless of the weariness of the day's march. They were patient, hard-working, bright, and eager to learn, and seeing them made you feel that China was not hopeless, that no nation was more hopeless than its youth. Here in the Vanguards was the future of China, if only this youth could be freed, shaped, made aware, and given a role to perform in the building of a new world. It sounds somewhat evangelical, I suppose, but nobody could see these heroic young lives without feeling that man in China is not born rotten, but with infinite possibilities of personality.

36

THE RAPE OF NANJING

JOHN POWELL

John Powell (1888–1947), an American journalist who lived in China for twenty-five years from 1917, was partly responsible for setting up the China Weekly Review *in Shanghai in 1923 and was for many years its editor. He continued to live in Shanghai even after the Japanese occupied it in November 1937, but with the bombing of Pearl Harbor in December 1941 his journal was closed down and he himself imprisoned. Not long afterwards he was included in an exchange of American and Japanese civilians, released, and repatriated.*

Powell's approach to China was typical of many Americans. He was generally extremely positive about the Nationalist Party and its main leaders, Sun Yat-sen and Chiang Kai-shek. He saw China through American lenses, meaning that he had faith in American policy towards China and in the behaviour of Americans in China. The missionaries, in particular, are portrayed as humane benefactors of China. Equally, Powell was fiercely anti-Communist and anti-Japanese.

Powell's book, My Twenty-five Years in China, *reads like a history of China from 1917 to 1942, with much emphasis on his own experiences. The following is his account of the Nanjing Massacre of December 1937. Although much has been written about this event, Powell's record has fascinating, if ghastly, details which emphasize the brutality and shamelessness of the Japanese troops. This excerpt is the first section of the chapter entitled 'American Ships, Japanese Bombs, in 1937'.*

After Japan's war in China had been in progress for several months, two young Japanese officers, former schoolmates at the Tokyo Military Academy, met in Nanking, capital of Nationalist China. Nanking had just fallen to the Japanese. The

Crowded street scene in Shanghai, 1930s. Photograph by Arthur Hodges. Courtesy of Joscelyn Burn.

time of the meeting was a few days before Christmas. The young officers were Sub-lieutenants Tashiakai Mukai and Iwao Noda. The meeting of the two officers in the Chinese capital was a matter of considerable popular interest in Japan as their exploits had been heralded, together with their pictures, in the daily editions of the Tokyo *Nichi Nichi Shimbun*, leading newspaper in the Japanese capital.

The following is a brief translation of the account of the meeting of the two Japanese officers in the Chinese capital, which a translator in my office handed me one morning: 'After formal bows the two Japanese officers drew their swords and pointed with pride to the badly nicked edges of the long blades. Said Lieutenant Noda, "I have killed 105—how many have you killed?" Lieutenant Mukai replied, "Aha-ha, I have killed 106—so sorry!" '

Mukai had won by one on a matter of points, but, the *Nichi Nichi's* correspondent explained, it was impossible to settle the bet between the two officers because there was no way of determining which of the two had passed the 100 mark first; it was therefore decided to call it a tie and extend the competition to determine which officer could pass the 150 mark, that is, kill 150 Chinese.

A dead Chinese man, 1930s. Photograph by Arthur Hodges. Courtesy of Joscelyn Burn.

The report in the Tokyo *Nichi Nichi* stated that the race 'started with renewed vigor December 11 for the goal of 150.' It appeared that the two officers had first met in a night club in Shanghai, when the original bet had been made to determine which of the two could first kill 100 Chinese. It was not specified that the victims had to be Chinese soldiers; as a matter of fact the Chinese army had withdrawn from most of the towns between Shanghai and Nanking, a distance of some 200 miles, through which the Japanese army advanced on its way to Nanking. It was assumed therefore that most of the victims of the competition in mass murder by the two Japanese officers had been Chinese civilians.

Some time after the occupation of Nanking on December 13, 1937, the Japanese army spokesman at Shanghai announced that the army had decided to establish a factory in Shanghai for the repair and reconditioning of swords.

The report of the competition of the two Japanese army officers shed considerable light on the orgy of looting, murder, and rape which took place following the entrance of Japanese troops into the Chinese capital. There had been some looting by the defeated and retreating Chinese troops, and Nanking had experienced serious rioting and disorder, with atrocities against Chinese civilians and foreigners, at the hands of the Communists in 1927, but the residents of the Chinese capital had never experienced such an ordeal as marked the occupation of the city by the Japanese army. Japanese occupation of the native sections of Shanghai and other cities of the lower Yangtze region had been accompanied by murder, looting, and the rape of civilians, and the Chinese generally were familiar with the stories of Japanese atrocities in Manchuria, where entire populations of villages had been wiped out and all of the houses looted and burned by the Japanese because the villagers were accused of harbouring guerrillas.

The rape of Nanking was almost like that of Carthage in the barbarity shown to its inhabitants. The account of foreign missionaries, many of whom had witnessed the atrocities, and even obtained pictures of them, indicated that there was a collapse of all discipline among a considerable section of the Japanese forces. It seemed as though all of the pent-up hatred for foreigners with which the Japanese army had been indoctrinated by years of teaching and training in brutality burst forth in an orgy of terrorism following the occupation of the city. An authenticated report by an international group of foreign missionaries stated that large numbers of Chinese civilians were wantonly shot or bayonetted and left to die in the streets. People who attempted to flee the city were rounded up, robbed, and machine-gunned indiscriminately. So-called safety zones which were created and supervised by missionaries were invaded by Japanese soldiers during the reign of terror, which continued for several days. Large numbers of men were bound together and shot in bunches, or their clothing was saturated with kerosene and they were burned to death as human torches.

The Japanese charged that the Chinese victims were soldiers who had discarded their uniforms for civilian attire and were trying to escape from the city. Japanese soldiers singled out 400 males of various ages from one refugee safety zone, which was supervised by Christian missionaries, and marched them outside the city wall in groups of fifty, to be mowed down by machine guns. Other Chinese were tied to posts and used as dummies for bayonet practice. Japanese soldiers invaded the premises of mission schools and seized Chinese women and girls, who were dragged away. Not a single prisoner was taken by the Japanese army. Japan's propaganda that her sole purpose was to 'liberate' the Chinese people was made to mean in actual practice their 'liquidation.' John Allison, an American consular official who accompanied a

Chinese victims of war. Photograph by Arthur Hodges. Courtesy of Joscelyn Burn.

missionary to the Japanese army headquarters for the purpose of urging the Japanese commander to control his rioting troops, was slapped and insulted by the Japanese sentry at the gates of the compound. Most of the private homes in the city were plundered, and refugees passing through the city gates were robbed of their meager possessions. . . .

I also saw numerous pictures snapped by the Japanese themselves, showing Chinese being beheaded by Japanese soldiers, and I possessed one revolting picture of a Chinese woman who had been raped by two Japanese soldiers who were shown in the picture standing by the body of their victim. The Japanese have a weakness for photographing each other, and could not resist photographing even their own barbarous acts. I obtained the prints from a Korean photograph shop in Shanghai, where the films had been sent to be developed. The soldiers apparently wanted the prints to send to their friends at home in Japan. Japanese soldiers seemingly had no feeling whatsoever that their inhuman actions transgressed the tenets of modern warfare or common everyday morals.

PART X

MAO'S UTOPIA

The Chinese Communist Party (CCP) won their war against Chiang Kai-shek in 1949 and set up the People's Republic of China (PRC), with Mao Zedong as President and Party Chairman. Although in its early years the regime carried out a social revolution, it also achieved significant economic advances. In 1966, Mao began his ultra-radical Cultural Revolution, which aimed to overthrow old-fashioned bureaucrats and bring China closer to a communist utopia, but which backfired catastrophically and damaged the country greatly.

Western reaction to the establishment of the PRC was generally extremely negative, both at government and popular levels. Outside the Communist bloc, Britain was the first Western country to establish diplomatic relations with the new regime, notifying Beijing of that intention on 6 January 1950. Until these relations were raised to ambassadorial level, in 1972, the British Office in Beijing was headed by a chargé d'affaires. France established full diplomatic relations with China in January 1964.

37

THE SUPREME DANGER

PEARL BUCK

Only a small number of Westerners lived in China in the 1950s and early 1960s. The United States government actually forbade its citizens to set foot on Chinese soil, though Pearl Buck, who lived the second half of her life in America, continued to feel strongly about China and wrote a great deal more about it.

Despite sharing with Mao Zedong an intense respect for the Chinese peasant, she was always bitterly anti-Communist. In the following passage, she spells out her thoughts just a few years after the CCP's victory and reflects on the nature of the Chinese revolution.

W hen it became clear to me that we had lost, as day after day the Nationalist armies surrendered without battle, handing over their American-supplied arms to the Communists, I spent much thought upon what could next be done. I had no blame in my heart for those yielding soldiers. Soldiers? They were not soldiers. Chiang's real army had been kept intact and would retreat with him to Formosa [Taiwan] as had been planned long before. No, the soldiers who faced the Communists were for the most part just country boys, sent in from the provinces upon order. . . .

No, there was no use by now in blaming anyone. The question remained, how could American democracy prevent Chinese Communism from following the harsh Soviet pattern? Much was in our favour. Mao Tse-tung, the acknowledged Communist leader of China, had never been really *persona grata* with Soviet Russia, or so one heard. At one time it was even rumoured that he had been expelled from the International Party for insubordination to Communist principle and discipline. Certainly he had followed a pattern of his own. Moreover, I could not believe that the good record of Americans in China for a hundred years had been

A street scene in Xian, capital of Shaanxi, 1965. Women hauling loads were quite a common sight in the Chinese provinces at the time. Photograph by Colin Mackerras.

forgotten. American boys living in China during the war had, it is true, left behind them mixed impressions. The intelligent and civilized ones were liked and became good ambassadors for their people. But many of them were not civilized and intelligent and being mere children in years, for what man is mature before twenty-five at least, they had acted like naughty boys, drinking too much and insulting women and sometimes behaving like criminals. I had grieved about this for a while, hearing directly as I did in those years from Chinese friends, and then I reflected that perhaps the time had come for the Chinese and the Americans to know each other exactly as we were, good and bad. On the whole, the record, I say, is good. . . .

In the intervening years of increasing tension and the outbreak of the Korean war [mid-1950], I pondered much upon the history of China in my lifetime. I have come to the conclusion at last that it is dangerous, perhaps the supreme danger, for persons or parties to destroy the framework of government which a people has built for itself, not consciously or by sudden choice, but by the slow and profound processes of life and time. The framework is the structure upon which people hang their habits and their customs, their religions and their philosophy. An old house can be changed and strengthened and remodeled and lived in for centuries if the essential framework holds. But once the whole structure is pulled down into dust it may never be rebuilt, and the people who lived in it are lost and wandering.

A revolution, therefore, inevitable in the history of any people when living conditions become intolerable, should always stop short of total destruction of the framework. Thus Sun Yat-sen, when in desperation he overthrew the Manchu dynasty, should not, I have come to believe, also have overthrown the form of government. The Throne should have been upheld, the system maintained, and within that framework reforms carried out. The Chinese people, like the British, were accustomed to a ruling figure. They had developed their own resistances to tyranny, and with increasing knowledge of Western democracy and its benefits they would have assumed modern manners of their own. The English system might have provided better guidance for them than ours. We are not an ancient people. The Chinese background is very different from ours.

This will seem a heretical conclusion, doubtless, not only for many westerners but also for a considerable number of Western-educated Chinese. Nevertheless, I maintain it. Sun Yat-sen was an honourable and selfless man, whose integrity is beyond doubt. He deserves the homage of his people. He is not to be blamed that in his burning desire to serve them he destroyed the very basis of their life, which was order.

It is dangerous to try to save people—very dangerous indeed! I have never heard of a human being who was strong enough for it. Heaven is an inspiring goal, but what if on the way the soul is lost in hell?

38

THE RED GUARDS CONDEMNED

JACQUES MARCUSE

One of the few Western journalists to live in China in the 1960s was Jacques Marcuse. He already had considerable experience of the country before the CCP came to power and regarded himself as an 'old China hand'. He left China just before the Cultural Revolution and wrote of his experiences in The Peking Papers, *the tone of which is indicated by its dedication: 'To the memory of Dr Pavlov's dog, this book is humbly dedicated by the Pekinese who wrote it'.*

Here Marcuse writes about the Red Guards [hong wei bing], and especially religion. The Red Guards were groups of young people mandated by Mao in 1966 to carry out the Cultural Revolution on his behalf. In that year Mao held several enormous demonstrations of Red Guards in Tian An Men (Gate of Heavenly Peace) Square, in the heart of Beijing, with himself and his deputy Lin Biao standing atop the Gate of Heavenly Peace. The Red Guards were disbanded in disgrace in the summer of 1968, most of them being sent to the countryside for ideological remoulding.

Some priests had been put to death with boiling water poured on their heads, others had been disemboweled, others still, crucified or buried alive. This latter form of execution is an old Chinese Communist practice of which I heard for the first time (not from Kuomintang sources) in 1940. As late as October 1966, the religious news agency KIPA reported that several Chinese Catholic priests had recently died that atrocious death (at the hands, I presume, of the Red Guards) in Tientsin [Tianjin], which is no more than 85 miles from Peking. What may have happened still farther away from foreign eyes, one can only guess. In Peking, Shanghai, and Canton [Guangzhou], frightening as their behavior

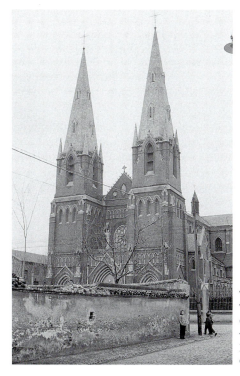

The Catholic cathedral in Tianjin, early 1965. Like all Catholic churches, this one was closed during the Cultural Revolution. Photograph by Colin Mackerras.

may have appeared to some, the Red Guards were still held on a tight rein. But in their activities, restricted as they were, a familiar pattern appears: the desecration of temples and cemeteries, the humbling of priests and 'bourgeois,' the burning of books. All of this strikes a chord in one's memory because it all happened in Tibet only seven years ago. There, too, religious symbols were plastered with pseudo-Communist slogans, by youths motivated not so much by the thinking of Mao Tse-tung or any understanding of Marxist-Leninist thumb-the-seam discipline, as by a sudden sense of their own importance.

Still, the real victims of the *hung wei ping* [*hong wei bing*] are ultimately bound to be the *hung wei ping* themselves. . . .

Once they have played their assigned part they will be sent to the country both to learn from the people and to teach the people and they will be swallowed up and not heard of again or they will be incorporated, willy-nilly, in the PLA [People's Liberation

Army]. They will have served their purpose, destructive as it will have been.

Yes, the Red Guards will become their own victims. But these victims will include a very illustrious person: Mao. And that is why I said that only a counsel of despair could have prompted Mao, or perhaps his deputy, his 'close comrade-in-arms' Lin Piao [Lin Biao], whose very violence is that of a very sick man with nothing much to lose, to conjure up the Guards. For if there is something that the Red Guards are *not* doing, it is spreading goodwill and pouring out the milk of human kindness by the bucket. And since they are doing everything they do on Mao's official behest, it is unlikely that the old Leader's popularity will be enhanced or that the shining beacon of his thought will acquire greater candle-power.

It is a strange picture that rises before my mind's eye at this juncture: old and sick Mao and younger but sicker Lin Piao standing together on the rostrum of Tien An Men [Tiananmen]. Night has fallen. They are alone. They are breathing *maotai* [strong Chinese spirit] into each other's face, for they have just finished dinner. From the city, ill lit but for Changan Avenue at their feet, comes, not the sound, but the silence of fear—for fear is noiseless. And silent they are, too, and it makes them a little uneasy. And they watch, just to do something, the water cart below that sprinkles the macadam, while the rainclouds, unseen, gather in the black sky overhead.

At the end of his book, Marcuse sums up his attitude towards China and the Chinese.

I have spent many happy years of my life in China. I have a great love for China and her people. I have many Chinese friends and indeed owe my life to some of them.

It may sound odd, coming from the lips of an 'old China hand' like myself who for a very long time enjoyed the one-sided advantages and amenities provided by the Unequal Treaties, but I will still say it: I do not like to see the Chinese humiliated. And I do not like the regime that humiliates them, much as I still admire some of its leaders for what they did in the past and for what they still are today.

But when, to the odium of totalitarian dictatorship and brainwashing, I find added comic and self-important imbecility, I see no reason to deny myself the relief of a chuckle. . . .

If, between the covers of this book, I have attempted to demystify China, it is not because I do not like China, but because I dislike a certain type of mystification and abominate a social system that founds its strengths on the deliberate and forcible vilification of the dignity of the human person and which it is now fashionable to overglamorize, overfear, and generally overrate.

39

FOREIGN EXPERTS

ERIC GORDON

In the mid-1960s, the Chinese government invited English teachers, technicians, and others from Europe to work in China. Among these people many were committed to the Chinese cause, but others were simply curious to find out how China was faring in the wake of the split with the Soviet Union. Many were ranked as 'foreign experts'. On the whole, the Westerners among this group formed a positive impression of China.

When the Cultural Revolution broke out, most foreign workers left China, their contracts having expired or the Cultural Revolution rendering them of no further use to the Chinese. Although shocked by the outbreak, most were not seriously harmed by it and some even became active supporters of the Cultural Revolution.

Several accounts survive written by Westerners who worked in China at that time. One is by Eric Gordon, who went with his wife Marie and son Kim to work in China. Both parents were dedicated socialists and very friendly to the People's Republic. Yet just as they were about to leave China, Eric was arrested and all three were kept in a single room for nearly two years. Why they were imprisoned was never made clear, but they were probably pawns in a power struggle. They were released in October 1969.

The following contains comments about the teaching work which Marie carried out before the Cultural Revolution, her students, and the institute where she worked.

Though I was feeling pretty frustrated with my work, the same could not be said of Marie. From the day she started teaching until she stopped nearly eighteen months later she was bound up with her work as never before. She seemed to spend every day thinking and talking about her students, worrying about their progress, planning future teaching programmes. The institute became a conversational topic to the exclusion of practically everything else: I almost became jealous of it. I could see why her students appealed to her. In class they were studious, respectful, and insatiably curious about the English language; out of the classroom, they were outgoing, warm, and responsive, far less sophisticated than English youngsters of the same age (they ranged between seventeen and twenty-five), and though neat and tidy in appearance they were not over-interested—boys or girls—in clothes and possessions. Nor did sex seem to pose any problems for them. They just appeared to take it for granted that it would come naturally enough after they had left college. Politically, they were mixed. Some were much less 'revolutionary' than others, having brought such luxuries as spring mattresses and radios from home. They also received a lot of pocket money from their parents which they would sometimes blow in one evening at an expensive restaurant. Others declared themselves the problem children of the family; older siblings were settled in parents' businesses, but they themselves, influenced by China's propaganda and with left-wing leanings, had begged to be allowed to go to their Utopia. They were almost desperately enthusiastic about everything Chinese—something like the long-term foreign residents whom we later dubbed 'Sunshiners' but with a far more natural and sincere fervour. Most wanted to be teachers, especially in China's backward countryside.

The institute, which lay just behind my office, occupied a large walled compound. Walls! I don't think you will find a school, college, office, or factory in Peking that isn't behind walls or high railings. The buildings were the usual dull grey stone blocks containing classrooms, dormitories—the students slept about ten to a small room—and an indoor swimming pool, interspersed with trees, bushes, and a large gravelled field where the two thousand students played games or did militia training, usually bayonet practice with wooden rifles.

40

A GREAT FRAUD

SIMON LEYS

TRANSLATED BY COLIN MACKERRAS

One of the fiercest Western opponents of the Cultural Revolution was the Belgian academic Pierre Ryckmans. He carried out extensive research on Chinese cultural history, especially painting, but when writing on contemporary China, Ryckmans generally adopted the pen-name Simon Leys because of his intense hatred for the Communist regime. The identity of Simon Leys quickly became known, yet he continued to use the pen-name.

The following passage, from the first of his major books on the Cultural Revolution, borrows its title from Hans Christian Andersen's story 'The Emperor's New Clothes'. Ryckmans believed the Cultural Revolution to be a total fraud, despite the fact that almost nobody dared call it such, and a power struggle by which Mao strove to regain power he had lost. Leys had no time at all for those in the West who sympathized with the Cultural Revolution.

The 'Cultural Revolution', which had nothing revolutionary about it other than its name, and nothing cultural except for the initial tactical pretext, was a *power struggle*, led *at the top* among a *handful of individuals*, behind the smoke-screen of a fictitious mass movement. (Following the event, because of the chaos engendered by this struggle, a genuinely revolutionary mass current did develop spontaneously at the grass roots, expressing itself in *military mutinies* and *enormous workers' strikes*. These, which were not planned as part of the programme, were put down ruthlessly.) In the West certain commentators persist in understanding the official label literally and take the notion of 'a revolution in culture' as their point of departure, and even 'a revolution in civilization' (the Chinese term *wenhua* does indeed allow for this ambiguity). In regard to so uplifting a theme, any attempt to reduce the phenomenon to so sordid and trivial a level as a 'power struggle' sounds wounding, even defamatory, to the ears of European Maoists. As for the Maoists of China, they have rid themselves of such delicacies: as a matter of fact, the definition of the 'Cultural Revolution' as a *power struggle (quanli douzheng)* is not an invention of the opponents of the regime, it is the official definition proposed by Peking and repeated constantly in the editorials of *People's Daily, Liberation Army Daily,* and *Red Flag* from the beginning of 1967 just when the movement was advanced enough to be able definitively to abandon the cultural smoke-screen behind which it had sheltered its first steps. It was difficult for European observers to admit that Mao Zedong had effectively *lost power.* But it was precisely to regain it that he launched this struggle. What is amazing is that it should still be necessary (after four years of 'Cultural Revolution'!) to go over the evidence again. But in fact, there are still specialists of contemporary Chinese politics in Europe and America who wish to downplay, put in doubt, or deny the fact that Mao had been pushed from power.

41

CITIZEN WANG

EDGAR SNOW

Simon Leys's view was widely accepted at the time. Yet a few Western observers were still impressed by what they thought Mao was doing. One of the most distinguished of these was Edgar Snow, author of Red Star Over China. *He had made several visits back to China after Mao and his CCP came to power, and his last book resulted from a visit he made to China in 1970–71, before United States President Richard Nixon's 1972 visit. By the early 1970s Snow was able to attempt an evaluation of the Cultural Revolution and the effect it had exerted on the lives of the Chinese people. In contrast to most commentators, his assessment is quite positive. As it happened, Snow did not finish this book, since he died in mid-February 1972, but his widow, Lois Wheeler Snow, had it published on his behalf. It came out in 1971 and, appearing to presage a new, more favourable view of China resulting from Nixon's accommodation, was reprinted several times.*

Citizen Wang, our man in the street, had grown neither horns nor a halo since 1965. 'Chairman Mao is always with us,' sang some small children to me in a factory kindergarten equipped with its own air-raid shelter—a new thing. Both they and their parents said they loved Mao, and there seemed little reason to doubt that most of them meant it. Yet except for the Mao badges worn by everybody, the outward appearance of citizens still closely resembled that of the man I had seen before the cultural revolution.

There was more uniformity of dress: blue and grey jackets and trousers, in the winter padded with cotton, for both men and women, with a greater mixture of army or militia khaki and navy pale blue. Except for their red-starred caps and red-barred collar tabs soldiers were indistinguishable from civilians. Many women

A baby in a barrel with his sister in a village just outside Hangzhou, capital of Zhejiang. This was a common way of looking after babies in Zhejiang in the 1960s. Photograph by Colin Mackerras.

wore brighter and better clothes at home, where nearly all had stored away a silk or woollen garment or two for special occasions, but the street fashion was now proletarian. . . .

Citizen Wang is now well fed, healthy, adequately clad, fully employed with labour tasks, Mao classes, and technical studies, during his six-day work week. On his free day—usually a Sunday but often a week day; free days are staggered to relieve congestion—he relaxes with his family or may play ping-pong or in summer swim in a pool or river or lake or the sea—and swimming is still a sport new to China. In winter he may join hikers in the countryside. He may also volunteer to dig holes and make bricks for air-raid shelters—working alongside a physician or a teacher. . . .

We cannot really see inside Citizen Wang, but if this man has worries they obviously do not include mounting food prices, medical costs, or taxes. Prices have been stable or declining for more than a decade and there is no inflation or black market. Wang pays no personal income taxes; State revenues derived from surplus labour value are hidden in the form of price controls in the state-managed market, which keeps consumption within planned necessity. Citizen Wang lives on a very narrow budget but is free from bank mortgages, debt, and the fear of starvation and beggary which plagued his parents.

His cultural life includes access to parks, playgrounds, museums, lectures, concerts, radio, television, and theatre for very small fees or none at all. In 1970 his choice of books was confined to textbooks and the works of Mao. He may own a long-wave radio or may buy parts for and assemble a short-wave set. In rare instances he may have television. The Box is relatively more expensive than abroad, and television sets are usually collectively owned by one's group or institution. All programmes are heavily larded with political propaganda, as in the theatre. Tickets for theatrical and sports events are in great demand, and in practice (although a very few seats are sold at the box office) are available only through one's group. Movies are plentiful and cheap but offer little variety.

The wall posters our friend reads carry Mao's directives or exhortations; the newspapers, generally scanned on public bulletin boards, convey only Party-line news. Foreign news is scant and carefully screened; one reads nothing to upset the view that China, thought still backward in many respects, is politically correct about everything. On the other hand, Mr Wang is not troubled by murder stories, market plunges, pornography, race riots, divorce scandals, dope rings, muggings, commercialized sex, sadism and masochism, and class envy of the rich. There are no more rich. There are also very few corrupt officials, thieves, or other parasites. Though class enemies still exist, they are mostly responsible for evils abroad.

In short, China is, as some wit has remarked before me, a veritable sink of morality.

42

A BRITISH DIPLOMAT REFLECTS

PERCY CRADOCK

One of Britain's most distinguished diplomats in China in the second half of the twentieth century was Sir Percy Cradock. From 1966 to 1969 he was Political Counsellor, then chargé d'affaires in Beijing, and later, from 1978 to 1984, ambassador. From 1984 to 1992, he was the British Prime Minister's Foreign Policy Adviser, in which capacity he conducted negotiations with the PRC, including those on the Hong Kong Joint Declaration of December 1984.

The following records his observations on the Cultural Revolution from 1966 to 1969, a period which marked the nadir of Britain's relations with China; on 22 August 1967, Red Guards occupied the British Office in Beijing and burned down the Chancery building. Cradock calls his chapter on the Cultural Revolution 'Reflections on a Disaster' and he notes that the Chinese themselves changed their mind about the Cultural Revolution— the CCP denounced it in June 1981.

From a purely professional point of view the Cultural Revolution, for all its horrors, had been a source of intense interest, a fascination. I had been a spectator at an immense and historical convulsion, a movement whose course I understood and which I could analyse and report and even, to some very small degree, predict. It was like having the French Revolution performed in the road outside and occasionally being required to join in. It had its dangers, but, for the historian, the student of Communism, or the sinologist, there were great compensations. They were increased by the access, via Red Guard posters and publications, to information normally closed to all foreigners and to virtually all Chinese. The workings of a Communist state and the manoeuvres within the Chinese body politic were briefly visible. If much of what one saw only served to confirm the darkest views of human nature, or to evoke cynical laughter, it was nevertheless a unique insight.

But outside this narrow professional context there was little to comfort or encourage. The country was in the grip of a nightmare, a regime under which the normal vices of a Communist system were swollen to monstrous proportions. The standard lies and persecutions were now on an Orwellian scale; the tyranny both complete and capricious; the link with reality almost non-existent. As the Han-dynasty historian wrote of the reign of terror under the first Emperor, Qin Shi Huang Di: 'The condemned were an innumerable multitude. . . . From the Princes and Ministers down to the humblest people everyone was terrified and in fear of their lives. No man felt secure in his office; all were easily degraded.'

Moreover, it was a regime whose energies were largely directed to destroying its own resources, political, intellectual, and economic. Under the strains it imposed, the downward potential of human nature was brutally exposed: one noted how rapidly respect had been turned into mindless adulation, criticism into torture and killing. There was only a short step from absurdity to atrocity.

It was impossible to avoid a deep sense of waste at the spectacle of the talents and devotion of a gifted people rejected or misused.

Children in a primary school in Beijing in the mid-1960s, with a portrait of Chairman Mao in the background. Photograph by Colin Mackerras.

Even in our confined world we had seen examples enough of personal shame and suffering: the doctors condemned to scrub the ward floors, the old amah with her long hair forcibly cropped, the Chinese office staff terrified of interrogation by students, or indeed of their own children, and one by one removed to be punished and re-educated, some to return, some not. We had seen ourselves a little of the beatings and vandalism. And outside this small circle there was the immense national suffering one could divine from the official statements, the posters, and the various reports available to us.

These self-inflicted wounds were too large to assess accurately. Though certain sectors seem to have been protected, notably those concerned with nuclear weapons, and agriculture came off lightly, the economy had slipped back several years, at a time when population growth made rapid progress critical. The Great Leap Forward was indisputably a major disaster; Chinese writers put the deaths resulting from it at twenty million. But the official Chinese judgement in 1981 placed the Cultural Revolution in a league of its own, as the greatest national catastrophe the Communist regime had had to endure: 'the most severe setback and the heaviest losses suffered by the Party, the state, and the people since the founding of the People's Republic'. The fatalities were much less than in the Great Leap and the associated famines; but the political and spiritual damage and scars were greater and longer-lasting.

43

CANNIBALISM

JOHN GITTINGS

Although horrific stories about China appeared in the Western press, it was rarely possible to confirm them. One set of particularly terrible reports concerned corpses showing the signs of torture, with hands tied, floating into Hong Kong's harbour in the middle of 1968.

John Gittings, a prominent British journalist and China specialist, filed many critical but also sympathetic reports about China for Hong Kong's Far Eastern Economic Review, The Guardian, *and other newspapers.*

In this extract, written nearly thirty years after the situation it describes, Gittings comments on alleged cannibalism in a place called Wuxuan, Guangxi, in May–June 1968. It is only the beginning of a detailed exposition which concludes that the ghastly report is indeed true.

Did they really eat people in China during the Cultural Revolution? Many people interested in China asked me this question after a dissident writer from Beijing had made the claim, a quarter of a century after the events were alleged to have taken place. Former 'friends of China' in the West were particularly upset. So many of their illusions about the Mao era had already been shattered: could this possibly be true as well? The writer Zheng Yi had brought out some convincing documentary evidence but there was only one way to be absolutely sure. That was to visit the town of Wuxuan where the most horrific and widespread cases were claimed to have occurred.

On the second morning I walked a few hundred metres from the guesthouse towards the old part of town. Beneath the covered market in Wuxuan's main square, sacks of rice and bundles of tobacco were being traded in an early morning grey mist. Peasant women from the Yi minority in broad-brimmed straw hats sat outside, with stacked tomatoes, piles of garlic, bundles of greens, and a few eggs laid out on a cloth before them. In spite of the occasion [National Day holidays], there was none of the variety of goods found in most Chinese markets these days: just a few piles of rubber sandals and some cheap clothes. Outside the department store a huckster from out of town selling sets of shoddy stereo speakers had attracted a crowd of poorly dressed young men.

The subject of cannibalism is not an easy one to raise even at such a distance from the alleged events. But within half an hour, I had secured an unambiguous answer. Mr Li, a friendly middle-aged government clerk, was surprised I had heard the story but eager to confirm it. (Li is not his real name, although he wrote it down readily enough—and his address—in my notebook.) 'Yes, it was really bad in Wuxuan,' he told me. 'Just over there'—he pointed towards the main street of the old town stretching behind the market—'I saw them. There was a big explosion next to the market and bodies everywhere.' But were people really eaten as well, I asked? 'Of course, they were; it's true, not false at all! In Wuxuan,' Mr Li added with a touch of pride, 'we ate more people than anywhere else in China!'

Gittings later states in Real China, From Cannibalism to Karaoke *that the savagery was part of a 'merciless class struggle' which Mao had prescribed for the whole country.*

163

PART XI

THE PENDULUM SWINGS AGAIN

T he early 1970s saw a major improvement in China's relations with the West. Beginning with Canada and Italy, a stream of Western countries recognized the PRC and established diplomatic relations with it. In July 1971, to international shock and surprise, United States President Richard Nixon announced his intention to visit China before May 1972. This announcement spawned a major improvement in American and other Western images of China. It became fashionable for Westerners to visit China, with the result that tourism mushroomed, as did television and radio reports and writings about personal experiences there. As one distinguished commentator put it, 'The diabolic, crude, ugly, inhuman, threatening Chinese were replaced by clever, charming, coping, attractive, hardworking Chinese'.[1]

44
ARE THE CHINESE DIFFERENT?

JOSEPH KRAFT

Nixon visited China, to enormous fanfare, from 21 to 28 February 1972, commenting that this was 'the week that changed the world'. He was accompanied by journalists and others; the television reporters beamed back generally favourable reports and the print journalists wrote correspondingly positive accounts of what they had seen.

An influential writer who accompanied Nixon was Joseph Kraft. He had worked for The New York Times and other publications, and even as a speechwriter for John F. Kennedy during the 1960 presidential campaign. At the time of Nixon's visit to China, Kraft, working in Washington, wrote a syndicated column which appeared in over 100 newspapers in the United States.

Kraft stayed on for a month or so after Nixon had left. He wrote a short book on his visit called The Chinese Difference, which was published later in 1972. In it he queries whether there is in fact a new Maoist man; had the Chinese succeeded in changing people, where the Soviet Union had so obviously failed to create a 'new Soviet man'? The following excerpt, from the end of the book, presents the author's answer. Although the passage is not entirely positive, the tone is clear that the Chinese 'difference' makes them better than others.

In the end, I suppose, the question I have posed respecting New Maoist Man has to be given a double answer. To a remarkable degree, the Chinese accept and observe the Maoist teachings. They do so in a disciplined fashion, obviously responsive to the pressure of the leadership. But that conformity must not be dismissed purely as a tactically smart response to Communist authority. Such disciplined conformity, for one thing, does not exist everywhere in the Communist world; it does not exist in the

Soviet Union. Moreover, many things learned by rote, and mouthed out of calculation, become in time the substance of true belief. To a large extent that seems to have happened in China. As the ambassador who was told on presenting his credentials that he was going to see a New Maoist Man said, 'Maoism is a kind of religion.'

Still, the Chinese believers are not old-time true believers. Fanatical devotion is curbed by the levity and skepticism of a cultivated people. I never saw a Chinese official strain, as Russian officials so often strain, to put a blatant act of self-interest within the ambit of the official line. Neither did I ever see a Chinese, after the fashion of so many Americans, show unease because behavior was not up to the standards of the ruling ethic. The Chinese know that their belief is a belief. They are supreme actors, mindful that somewhere there is a line between what is theatre and what is real, what is art and what is life. That self-consciousness, that ability to be pragmatic about belief, to use a religion, is what sets the Chinese apart from everybody else. It is the Chinese difference.

Premier Chou En-lai [Zhou Enlai], the most notable flesh-and-blood exemplar of the Chinese difference, made the point himself at a private dinner he gave for the President and his staff after the visit to the Great Wall. In his toast the premier cited a poem by Mao written around the Chinese proverb that 'to see the Wall is to become a man.' The tone seemed lukewarm, and afterward one of the Americans said to Chou, 'Mr Prime Minister, you give me the impression you're not really sure that we went to the Great Wall today.'

Chou replied, 'You have a very Chinese mind.'

45

A NEW SPIRIT

HARRISON E. SALISBURY

An even more influential journalist than Kraft was Harrison Salisbury. A long-time observer of the Soviet Union, he won the Pulitzer Prize and other awards for his reports from there. He also won prizes for reports from Vietnam and other places near to China. At the time of the Nixon visit Salisbury was a senior reporter with The New York Times.

Salisbury made his first visit to China in May 1972. Like Kraft he was concerned with the problem of the 'New Chinese Man' and he, too, wrote a book on his experiences, which was published shortly afterwards. His book is larger and more thoughtful than Kraft's, but also more concerned with himself and his own thoughts and conversations. The following extract comes near the end of the book and summarizes his impressions.

I n a word, China had lost some of its color, some of its street life, some of its diversity, some of its craftsmanship for the sake of an egalitarian life, for the sake of a life in which no one was very rich, no one was very poor, no one lived luxuriously, no one lived in want. The thrill and excitement of the Hong Kong streets could not be matched in Shanghai.

But there was a new China, there was a new life. Part of it had come into being with the Revolution in 1949. That laid the foundation. Then, in some manner, the Cultural Revolution, with its turbulence, its fighting, its conflict, its passion, its argument, its *luan* [chaos], had completed the process. There *is*—at least for a time—a New Chinese Man and a New Chinese Woman. They had stood up. They had self-respect and dignity. They were admirable in their fellowship, kindness, and sense of self-sacrifice. I admired them but I did not think they were for export, or that their spirit could simply be imitated in the United States, or anywhere else. It was as specifically Chinese as Chairman Mao's poetry.

Before I left China, I talked about this with a rather high official. We had been speaking of the Soviet Union. He—like every Chinese—was fascinated at my observations of Russia. I had said that it seemed to me that Russia had lost the spark of its Revolution. That it had been overtaken by materialism. The young people chased western fads like butterflies—the latest song, the latest dance, the latest style. Hippy clothing. Hippy haircuts. Drugs. They were trying to ape the western drug culture. It was hard to see what remnants of the Revolution were left. Soviet foreign policy differed hardly an iota from czarist foreign policy. I could not but feel that when the Chinese called the Soviet rulers the 'new czars' they had touched a very elemental truth.

But in China, there was something new. I agreed with those who said that the greatest change in China was in the spirit of the people.

The Chinese official smiled. They had made only a start. The task that China now faced was to turn her spiritual force into a material force. It was a great task, and China was only at its beginning. China was still very backward. He was sorry that I had not known the old China so that I could measure it by my own yardstick.

'I'm sorry, too,' I said. 'But nonetheless I think it is the miracle of the modern world.'

'Perhaps,' he said gently, 'you are going a bit too far.'

'No,' I replied, 'I don't think I'm going too far. I think that it is a great achievement to put a man on the moon. But to put a man on the earth—that is even more.'

The official smiled. He did not deny my statement. But he added a word of caution. 'If we lag in our efforts,' he said, 'we will slip back. We must move ahead. The time is still very short.'

He turned to the United States. 'Whatever your opinion of Nixon, or our opinion,' he said, 'he has done one thing right—China. Now it is up to the people—the people in both China and America. There is so much to be done. But no matter how long it will take, we think it can be achieved. The people will do it. The people of China and the people of America. They cannot be resisted.'

I agree with that. The peoples of America and of China—if they joined their strength—would be irresistible. I wished that I could feel more confident that they actually would come together in a human torrent that would sweep the world toward a better life. But I had reservations.

One area of great controversy in the West from the time of their establishment in 1958 was the rural people's communes. The following are Salisbury's observations about the communes. Like his overall impressions of China, they are strikingly positive and uncritical.

Contrary to all of the propaganda I had heard about Chinese 'blue ants,' and communes in which men and women lived in the same barracks, wore the same clothes, shared the same meals from the same wooden bowls, I found the hallmark of the Chinese commune to be diversity, local autonomy, total adjustment to local conditions, free and easy interchange between the team and brigade leaders and the membership, individual houses, individually farmed plots, individually owned animals and poultry (in addition, of course, to the commune plots), extraordinary diversity from one commune to another, and remarkable absence of interference from Peking and the provincial centres and peasants were free to sell surplus private production on the market.

I don't want to suggest that conditions were idyllic in the communes, or that politics was absent. They were not. And I encountered in some communes a number of experienced political workers who had been transferred into the communes to give better leadership, to ginger up production. But basically, the commune leadership was local, was intimately knowledgeable about the land it was tilling and the crops that were being grown.

What, then, had been added by the Communists? First and foremost, a convenient means for organizing the countryside and the peasant work force for more efficient labour, simultaneous action to carry out the laborious processes of seeding and harvesting. Then, of course, there was the great gift of health through the virtual elimination of epidemic disease; the elimination of the ruinous burdens of taxes and interest; the gradual introduction of better strains of seed and of improved fertilization (utilization under sanitary conditions of human fertilizer and provision of processed fertilizer in ever-increasing amounts); and the provision of technical aid and capital for large-scale irrigation projects that often made the difference between life and death in the arid areas of China.

46

THE NEW MOOD

JOHN SERVICE

Academic work and research on China expanded greatly because it became much easier to visit China and to carry out detailed research there. Although academic work retained its critical approach, the overall direction of research was considerably more positive about China in the 1970s than it had been in the 1950s or 1960s. The younger generation of scholars, who leaned towards the left, enjoyed more opportunities for research in China in the 1970s, when most of them began publishing their works.

One specific area of their work was the encyclopedia. Written by groups of specialists, brought together by expert editors, these encyclopedias also reflected the more positive, friendly approach to China characteristic of the 1970s. A good example is the Encyclopedia of China Today *by Frederic Kaplan, Julian Sobin and Stephen Andors, which aimed to provide up-to-date information about contemporary China.*

The Introduction to this encyclopedia was written by John Service. Born in Chongqing, Service lived in the CCP headquarters of Yan'an towards the end of World War II as part of an American delegation. His reports were much more sympathetic to the CCP than the prevailing American attitudes. He was among those dismissed from the State Department as a result of the purges orchestrated by Senator Joseph McCarthy in the 1950s, and it was alleged that he had contributed to the CCP's victory in China. Here he comments on China in the late 1970s, on Sino–US relations, and on the need for understanding.

I f China is now turning away from some of the policies of the Cultural Revolution and moving in different—if not entirely new—directions, the need is all the greater for a timely attempt—like this—to take a careful, objective, overall look that can provide a sort of benchmark, a measuring post for the future.

But the utility of realistic knowledge and understanding has even greater and more long-range significance. We Americans have consistently blundered and missed the boat in coping with the emergence of China as a world power. In 1945, our leaders ignored the facts we knew. In 1950, we had cut ourselves off from the facts. In the years leading up to the Vietnam War, we looked at the facts through coloured glasses and so saw them in distorted form.

China today is a peaceful but dynamic nation, central to the affairs of East Asia, especially influential in the Third World, and a nuclear power that can no longer be ignored in the world strategic equation. The policies that China adopts will clearly have a major impact on the prospects for stability and world peace. Those policies, in turn, will obviously be influenced by the policies that other powers pursue toward it. Those other powers include, perhaps most importantly, the United States. Our establishing—or rejecting—a stable, viable, and 'normal' relationship with the People's Republic of China cannot but have a broad effect on American interests, both regional and global. So far we have not yet, as a nation, come to grips with this issue.

A thoroughly and realistically informed public opinion has always been and still remains the best and only basis for a sound and credible American foreign policy. There is no substitute for plain, unvarnished facts. I hope and expect that this book will make a useful contribution to that end.

47

BAREFOOT DOCTORS

FREDERIC KAPLAN, JULIAN SOBIN, AND STEPHEN ANDORS

The 'barefoot doctor' system, a product of the Cultural Revolution, saw a large number of paramedics spread throughout the countryside. Stressing mass involvement over expertise, the barefoot doctors were noted for their ideological commitment and service to the people, as well as for their poor technical expertise and insufficient equipment. Yet they performed a very useful role in handling the peasantry's commonest ailments and were particularly active in spreading knowledge about birth control. Reaching its height in the 1970s, the network of barefoot doctors disintegrated under the pressures of the privatization of medicine in the 1980s and 1990s.

Expansion of Rural Services

Before the Cultural Revolution, however, people in the countryside had little, if any, day-to-day access to medical service; but since 1966, local and particularly rural medical services have been decentralized and rapidly expanded to help redress this problem. A large force of health personnel has been recruited from among the peasant and worker populations: 'barefoot doctors'—who also serve as agricultural workers in the communes and receive work points for both activities; 'worker-doctors'—who function in the industrial area on the same basis; and unpaid Red Medical Workers, who are usually housewives in urban neighbourhoods. Since such medical personnel undergo only brief formal training—usually three to six months in a hospital, with a series of follow-up refresher courses—the level of proficiency is uncertain, but compensation has been sought in attempts to provide continuing education at regular intervals.

As the program functions today, these practitioners can diagnose and treat simple illnesses, and refer to fully trained doctors those cases which they cannot handle. According to both official and observational accounts, great progress has been made in the availability of medical services. By 1973, the ratio of formally trained doctors to population was 1:5,000, and that of barefoot doctors to population, 1:7,000; in 1949, by contrast, there was a physician-population ratio of 1:13,000 (high estimate) or 1:100,000 (low estimate).

The emphasis on preventive medicine is now common all the way down to local networks of medical care. During 1949–65, when curative services still predominated and were concentrated in urban areas, a core of public health workers trained by the state worked out of a network of epidemic prevention centres, also mostly located in cities. These centres disseminated information on contagious diseases and administered mass immunization campaigns. Prior to 1958, only maternal child care, among the modern programmes, was geared to rural areas. Since the decentralization policy began in 1965, all health personnel in a locality have participated together in delivering preventive medical services. Such services have thus become responsible not only for treating individual patients but for overseeing the general well-being of entire communities.

48

STILL UNIMPRESSED

SIMON LEYS

Simon Leys (Pierre Ryckmans), as noted in Chapter 40, pronounced the Cultural Revolution a fraud. In 1972, by which time he held an academic post at the Australian National University in Canberra, he returned to China for about six months and wrote his impressions in a book which was published in his native French in 1974 and three years later in English.

Leys was not in the least impressed by the change in attitude towards China which followed the Nixon diplomacy. Indeed, he became well known throughout the Western world, and in China itself, for his hostility towards the Communist regime. In the following extract Leys compares China in 1955 and 1972. He does not identify the American journalists guilty of 'toadying flattery', but those already cited previously in this part may, for him, belong in that category.

I visited the People's Republic of China for the first time in 1955. I now return after seventeen years. The difference that strikes me the most—I speak here of purely visual, intuitive, superficial impressions, not taking into account the objective achievements that have been attained in the intervening years, which are certainly considerable—the difference that strikes me the most is that in 1955 everything seemed new, full of youth and life, and now everything seems old, run-down, ramshackle. Canton [Guangzhou] gives one a feeling of *déjà vu*; it's like another Macao—a significant comparison for anyone who knows that dirty obsolete old backwater. This impression grows in the north, where the cities cannot hide their tawdriness behind the luxuriance of tropical foliage. The buildings that date from after the Liberation of 1949 have not grown old gracefully: ersatz barracks, they become leprous after a few years. Housing clearly has a much lower priority than industrial infrastructure; also, the political climate does not encourage people to smarten up their flats or houses: better not give rise to neighbourly envy; better not live in a way that might be qualified as 'bourgeois'; any individual initiative to make daily life more pleasant or agreeable may bring suspicion or cause criticism. The wise man lives in a hovel and sews patches onto his trousers.

Others will say that the difference between 1955 and 1972 is not so much in what is seen as in who is doing the looking; in seventeen years one grows older and sourer. But I am struck by the opinion of many Chinese, based on personal experience and deep observation, that the regime was making great strides until 1956–57, only to see its forward dynamism compromised by the Hundred Flowers crisis [1957], and then broken for good by the failure of the Great Leap Forward [1958].

I can listen patiently and courteously when Chinese bureaucrats drone on with the trite sayings of Maoist propaganda: after all, they are only doing their job. But patience begins to fail me when the same old propaganda is served forth by Japanese diplomats or American journalists; the toadying flattery to which they have lowered themselves must sometimes turn the stomach of those they want to please. . . .

One should not misunderstand the melancholy recollections found here and there on the preceding pages. I would forgive *all* iconoclasms (I would welcome them with enthusiasm!) coming from a political power that was truly *of the people*—revolutionary, creative, opening up the ways of the future. But the present regime in China has destroyed the cultural and human values of the past only to retain its vices; it prolongs in its own interest the habits of feudalism and military bureaucracy. The psychology and political methods of the few old men who run China today derive directly from the Empire.

In Peking [Beijing], the only Chinese whom foreigners have a chance to get to know are their own servants. This faithfully repeats the colonialist situation, but now the fault is with the Chinese authorities themselves. It is typical that the regime has deliberately re-created all the features of that grotesque and shameful system, with its International Club, its segregated pleasures and shops, its ghetto.

In a postscript to his book, Leys tells the reader his view about the distinction between the government and people in China.

This book is at the opposite pole from the one I would wish to write—and one day hope I can write.

If the Maoist bureaucrats could only shed some of the pessimism, suspicion, and contempt with which they look down on those over whom they rule, and if they would only take a risk and let us live, truly live, among the people, I cannot believe that the experience would furnish such negative impressions as mine here. Not that the daily life of the Chinese people is such a picnic—far from it—but at least its inexhaustible humanity would be enough to wash the sterile sarcasm from these pages.

PART XII

A MODERN BACKLASH

The CCP formally approved Deng Xiaoping's reform and modernization programme at the end of 1978. The 1980s saw radical changes in China's society and economy in the direction of greater openness, freedom, and prosperity, though at no time did the CCP show any willingness to give up power. This became most obvious during the night of 3–4 June 1989, when the military in Beijing crushed student demonstrations that favoured freedom and democracy.

Until this crisis, the 1980s were generally a good period in relations between Western countries and China. The United States formally established full diplomatic relations with the PRC on 1 January 1979. The number of resident American journalists increased, student exchanges mushroomed, and academics could undertake field research in China to an unprecedented extent.

49

SMALL BACKLASH

FOX BUTTERFIELD

In the early period after normalization of diplomatic relations, quite hostile accounts of conditions in China persisted. John Service commented that, in the late 1970s, the positive image generated since the Nixon visit of 1972 appeared 'to have inspired its own small backlash, part reaction to knee-jerk enthusiasm and part hankering for a falsely idyllic past and for a Western concept of individualism that China's long history never generated.'[1]

Service's political opponents would not have accepted his formulation of the reasons for this 'small backlash'. But one who might be categorized among writers belonging to this backlash was Fox Butterfield, who was the resident correspondent for The New York Times *in the period immediately following the establishment of diplomatic relations between the United States and China. He claims that, having studied China at the suggestion of famous Harvard Professor John King Fairbank (1907–91), he learned the craft of journalism with* The New York Times *and then undertook assignments in Vietnam, Japan, and Hong Kong, 'waiting for China to open its doors to US news organizations'. He was thus 'ready to go' to Beijing when relations were finally established.*

The title of Butterfield's book, China, Alive in the Bitter Sea, *comes from an ancient Buddhist adage about survival in a world of suffering. The author points out that the Chinese revived this adage 'to describe their experience during the Cultural Revolution'. Indeed, the Cultural Revolution looms over this book as a nightmare. Ironically, official China was also reaching the same conclusion while Butterfield was working in China. This is obvious from the fact that the Sixth Plenum of the Eleventh Central Committee of late June 1981 formally condemned virtually everything about the Cultural Revolution, as well as Mao Zedong's action in initiating it.*

Although the Cultural Revolution is the ultimate nightmare, Butterfield also criticizes the present. In the following passage he sums up China's political economy under Deng Xiaoping, the main political leader of the 1980s.

For all the disaffection and cynicism of China's young people, the demoralization in the Party, and the rise of problems like crime, unemployment, and inflation, I had no sense that the Communists' hold on China is in danger. For one thing, their control apparatus, with its police, the *danwei* [unit] organization, the street committees, and political study, remains intact. For another, China is such a vast country that it took even the Communists thirty years to succeed in their revolution despite having a nation that was torn raw by foreign invasion, famine, banditry, and total economic collapse.

But most important, despite all the discontent, the Chinese are in no mood for more disruption. To borrow Richard Nixon's phrase, there is a silent majority of Chinese who want nothing more than the political stability and economic prosperity that Deng himself yearns for. . . . Almost no one wants a return to the Maoist style of mass movements and organized enthusiasm which they are afraid is the alternative to Deng and his program.

50

FROM THE CENTER OF THE EARTH

RICHARD BERNSTEIN

Ideology was especially rigid during the Cultural Revolution, and the narrowest form of Marxism–Leninism was imposed with no possibility of even mild deviations. In the 1980s, the lifting of this ideology saw a religious revival, in which Western writers took a keen interest. The religion to arouse the greatest interest was Christianity.

The following extract summarizes the situation for religion in the late 1970s and early 1980s. It is by journalist Richard Bernstein who, before writing his book From the Center of the Earth, The Search for the Truth about China, *worked in China for* Time *magazine. In the book Bernstein makes no secret of his strong opposition to the Communist regime. However, he also regards the Chinese as a lovable people. The last sentence of the book, about a female friend of Bernstein's, expresses his overall attitude: 'Just like the other lovable Chinese that I knew, she deserved more, more of a chance to be herself, more of an opportunity to contribute to the country that she continued, despite everything, to love, more of a chance to hope that after these decades of decline, of misdirection, of mediocrity, China might one day be great again.'*

There was no doubt, however, that by 1979 religion of all sorts, Buddhist, Moslem, and Christian, was flourishing in a new period of toleration. By mid-1981, more than forty Catholic churches had been retrieved from the schools, factories, and offices to which they had been turned over in 1966. There were Buddhist temples in every district. They became tourist sights. Over eighty Protestant churches had reopened as well as a Protestant seminary in Nanking [Nanjing] complete with forty bright, eager young students. If you bothered to look, you would find in practically any city in China, as I did in Chungking

[Chongqing], some rubble-strewn old church filled with workmen busily restoring it. I went to Lanzhou in northwestern Gansu Province and asked if, by any chance, there was a church. I was directed to the municipal library, a series of low-slung stone buildings around a courtyard. There, two hundred thousand books were being put into boxes and moved out so that the library, which before 1966 was the Protestant church, could become the Protestant church again. There was also a feeling of momentum in this, a sense that religious faith, after all that desiccated Maoist pseudointellectualism, was touching many new Chinese hearts. Even Pan Xiao [a young woman who in 1980 had contributed to a debate in the magazine *China Youth* on 'the meaning of life'] had gone to church and thought of becoming a nun. And, in Peking [Beijing], I met a number of young people who, while not actually going to church, were attracted to the notion of spiritual beliefs. Once in the Nationalities' Palace discotheque, I was talking to the pretty Chinese girl I used to dance with from time to time. 'Communism puts so much emphasis on struggle,' she told me when, for some reasons, the conversation turned to religion. 'What I like about Christianity is that it centres on kindness in human relations.'

But while, by their lights, China's leaders were making sincere efforts to respect once again the article on freedom of religion that was present in every Chinese constitution, it was freedom of religion on terms that still posed serious choices for individual believers. The churches were organized along the lines that were created in the 1950s, the Protestants into the so-called Three Self Christian Patriotic Movement, the Catholics into the Chinese Patriotic Catholic Association, the Buddhists into a Buddhist Association, and so on. For the Catholics, this meant no official contacts with the Holy See. It also meant remaining at best silent on such questions as abortion, divorce, and birth control where the policies of the state and of the church would normally have clashed. . . .

I do not wish to imply disrespect for those religious figures who decided to accept the 'patriotic' associations required by the party. At the very least, a decision to compromise allowed the churches to exist, so that these days, from Canton in the southeast to Urumchi in the northwest, Christian hymns do rise into the officially atheistic air of China. A religious figure could well argue that circumscribed churches are better than no churches at all, that it is better for Christian believers to have a place to worship on Sunday than not to have such a place. Once I talked with the Protestant bishop of China, Ding Guangxun, a former head of the World Christian Federation in Geneva, who is now the president of the Nanking [Nanjing] Theological Seminary. He argues forcefully and persuasively that only by putting the churches into the patriotic associations could the church leaders free Christianity from the stigma of being a foreign religion, that only in this way could the church be both fully Christian and fully Chinese.

And yet, what about those who did not compromise, who refused to see in religious belief any need for the Communists' ritual of fealty? Interested in the courage of conviction, I tended to put them on a different level from those who accepted the government's transformation of the churches. Moreover, unlike the impressive and forthright Bishop Ding, many a 'patriotic' churchman's pro-government rationalizations were so obsequious as to be devoid of all moral content.

51

THE POPULATION PROBLEM

ELIZABETH WRIGHT

Overpopulation proved a pressing problem during the 1980s. The government's response was to institute a policy that couples could have only one child. This decision aroused intense controversy in the West. The following sympathetic approach comes from a book written to accompany a series of programmes about China and its contemporary history. Entitled The Chinese People Stand Up, *the series was broadcast over the British Broadcasting Corporation (BBC) World Service and Radio 4.*

The author, Elizabeth Wright, had first been to Beijing in 1972 in the late stages of Mao's reign but actually wrote this book in the shadow of the 1989 political crisis.

One must have some sympathy with the present Chinese government and its attempt to limit the Chinese population, for they inherited another of Mao Zedong's mistakes. Mao had always declared that there could not be too many Chinese and any attempt to control the population was a Malthusian nonsense. Now the Chinese have a population of over 1100 million people. Earlier prognostications that the population would be 1.2 billion by the turn of the century have already been discarded, and it is admitted that it will be at least 1.3 billion. The population is growing by 20 million per annum, and a growth rate of that order requires nearly 7 million tons of grain each year to feed it. With 20 per cent of the world's population to feed from less than 5 per cent of the world's arable land, small wonder that the government is anxious.

Although the birth-control policy has been largely successful in the cities, where tiny flats and financial penalties are a great inducement to people to limit their families, the government admits that it has failed in the countryside. It is now acknowledged that local officials have lied about statistics, and that far more children are being born than was earlier realized. Now the government has relaxed the policy, and accepts that under certain conditions families may have a second child. For example, if both parents are only children, and their first child is a girl, then they may try for a second. But no one is supposed to have a third child. This is simply bowing to the inevitable, but it is also over-optimistic, as large numbers of rural families have produced three or more children despite the ban. If a rich family is fined for producing a second or third child, it gladly pays up, and the poor families feel that they are already so poor they have little to lose. Although the population growth is a major problem for China, at least the present relaxation should mean fewer cases of female infanticide and abortion of female foetuses.

52

FAMILY AND THE ECONOMY

CAROLINE BLUNDEN AND MARK ELVIN

The family situation and economic life are summed up briefly in the following passage, which refers to the 1980s but takes account of the whole period of the PRC to that time. The authors are Caroline Blunden, a specialist on Chinese painting, especially mural painting, and Mark Elvin, a British historian of China. It is part of an expensive, handsome coffee-table book, covering the whole of Chinese history, which has achieved considerable popularity.

The evidence suggests that family bonds are still extremely strong, though school indoctrination of children has obliged parents to be wary of what they say or do in their presence.

In recent times the Chinese family have moved in contrasting directions. In the countryside of the People's Republic, most of the housing is still in private hands. This confers substantial power on the older generation, as a properly functioning household economy is essential for a tolerable life. The choice of marriage partners still lies mainly with the parents, but the young people have a right of veto. The relationship between mother-in-law and daughter-in-law has subtly changed: the daughter-in-law needs the grandmother to look after her small children if she is to go out and work in the collective economy. Conversely, her greater earning power now gives her an enhanced status relative to the old lady, in comparison with earlier times. Having children brought up by their grandparents is a way, ironically, of filling them with old-fashioned values.

In the urban economy, married couples do not usually live with or near the man's parents, but pay jointly for their own accommodation. Choice of partners tends to be initiated by the young themselves, but is subject to a degree of veto by the parents and cadres in the units in which they work. There is little economic interdependence between the generations. The children are looked after in collective nurseries. This produces a type of character that places great emotional reliance on the peer-group (rather than elders), and is thus different from that of the rural child. The regimentation in the nursery schools is reported to be awesome, with naps and toilet-training all being taken together at particular times.

There has been growing state pressure over the last decade to limit the number of children. This has culminated in the policy of the one-child family, with reductions in welfare benefits and other sanctions for those who disobey. Women who work in factories are sometimes even assigned the year in which they may have their permitted child. Clearly, if this policy is successful, it will undermine what remains of the male descent-line mystique, since in any generation half the families will have no male heir.

53

UNDERSTANDING THE BODY AND THE UNIVERSE

ALASDAIR CLAYRE

A comprehensive BBC television series about China, The Heart of the Dragon, *focused on contemporary period but covered the past as well. First screened in the early 1980s, it was shown later in many different countries and was translated into a number of different languages. The following passage, from the book by Alasdair Clayre that accompanied the series, concerns health in China and shows the relationship between the past and present. The terms yin and yang are defined as 'pairs of fluidly interacting opposites, such as shadowed and bright, decaying and growing, moonlit and sunlit, cold and hot, earthly and heavenly, or female and male.'*

I n the early twentieth century, many thinkers in China rejected traditional Chinese medicine, along with other aspects of the Chinese past, as 'the accumulated garbage of several thousand years'. Sun Yat-sen, the founding father of the Republic, was himself trained at a Western medical college, as was China's greatest twentieth-century writer, Lu Xun. Western medicine was only beginning to make an impact in China at the time and until then had in any case had few effective therapies to offer. It was when the newly discovered germ theory of disease was applied to the Manchurian Plague of 1910–11 by Western doctors that their approach, with its 'specific' treatments as opposed to the Chinese 'holistic' way of understanding the body, began to be appreciated. It was at about the same time that some Western surgeons were tentatively accepted in China.

As the twentieth century went on, tides of opinion moved in different directions. The communists were attracted by the modernism of Western medicine, but in the 1930s and 1940s, while their bases were blockaded by the Nationalists, they discovered the value of traditional remedies as a means of treating their wounded when Western drugs were unobtainable. Some of their leaders were attracted to Chinese medicine as a store-house of national wisdom. When the communists came to power they increased training in both traditional and Western medicine, and a network of clinics and hospitals, which had been started in the 1920s and 1930s, was extended across the country.

Most production brigades now have rudimentary clinics, as do many neighbourhood and street committees in the cities. The pattern is far from uniform, and in the rural areas access to a hospital is often difficult. In addition, 'barefoot doctors', now called 'rural paramedical workers', with some two years' training in traditional and Western medicine, are available to treat the sick in the villages, and may also staff small country hospitals. They are no longer expected to work part-time in the fields.

In Chinese hospitals the responsibility for feeding the patients is often left in the first instance to their families. In some cases, only those without families are fed by the hospital. The Chinese consider that what one eats is an important factor in health and neither in Chinese medical thinking nor in the lore of folk healing is there any sharp distinction between what counts as food and what counts as medicine: the same verb, *chi*, means to ingest both food and medicine. Different kinds of food have different properties: some are yang, some yin, and ordinary people are usually well aware of the difference and treat minor ailments accordingly. Fresh ginger, which is yang, may be eaten to treat diarrhoea and stomach-ache, thought to be induced by anything yin or 'cold', from a draught to an icy drink. Dandelions and turnips, which have yin properties, may be eaten for boils, pimples, mouth ulcers, or abscesses, which are caused by 'heat'. One young Chinese remembers as an adolescent rubbing the family rhinoceros horn on a file about a foot long and tipping the horn powder into a bowl for her mother in Shanghai, who took the powder with a sip of tea whenever her migraine became intolerable. Once when she herself was suffering from a severe headache she asked her mother's permission to take some of the white powder, but was refused: unmarried girls were not allowed to use rhinoceros horn since its very powerful cooling effects, unbalanced by the yang of contact with a man, could cause sterility.

54
SUPERVISED FREEDOM

MARIE-CLAIRE BERGÈRE

TRANSLATED BY COLIN MACKERRAS

French China-watchers and sinologists commented extensively on China in the 1980s and were very much part of an international community in which the United States was the main partner.

The following commentary on China's social situation in the mid-1980s comes from a French modern historian of China, whose work on the early stages of the Chinese bourgeoisie is acknowledged as path-breaking.

Like all reforming regimes, Deng Xiaoping's is coming up against the difficulties inherent in granting more freedom but at the same time refusing complete freedom. It thus runs the risk of alienating the old elites without attracting new ones to its side. In exchange for involvement in the modernization effort, Beijing's rulers are allowing Chinese society some freedom . . . but supervised. They have allowed religious followers to practise their particular religion. Since 1980, thousands of Catholic churches and nearly a dozen seminaries have reopened. But priests are still subject to sanctions, as are believers who refuse to adhere to the official patriotic Church but submit to Vatican authority. The great Buddhist monasteries have also been restored. Once again, they attract crowds of faithful: 10,000 of them gathered at the Labrang Monastery in Gansu early in 1986. But the Dalai Lama, the religious head of the Tibetan community, has never tested this policy of tolerance by returning from exile. . . .

Far from having found an autonomous role, public opinion is still kept hostage to political factions and used for their ends. The free space which the reforms have reintroduced into Chinese society has, to be sure, affected the functioning of the regime, which has passed from totalitarianism to tempered authoritarianism. But the freedoms conceded are too limited, the society where they operate is too suffused with traditions to allow a real opposition to develop, a counter-power which can command the respect of the organs of authority.

By way of compensation there is a risk that, strong through its cultural heritage, society will successfully subvert these organs. The system of personal relationships (*guanxi*), which has staged a comeback thanks to liberalization, threatens socialist morality and competes with the exercise of bureaucratic authority. This system knows nothing of the values which form the basis of communist ideology: the Party, the state, the collective. It is foreign to the rules and regulations which organize the functioning of social life. The strands of family and regional solidarity flow round and through these rules and regulations, as well as the routes of escape from them. How can one superimpose two such contradictory systems on one another? For the regime, the risk of opening up society is less to throw the country onto the capitalist road than it is to plunge it back into divisions, particularisms, and backwardness.

Bergère's summative questions on the Chinese revolution and its future, seen from the vantage point of the mid-1980s, are also worth quoting.

Will the 1949 revolution dwindle in importance in our historical horizon, just as mountains seem lower the further we get away from them? It has been greeted as one of the century's upsets, as the equal of the French Revolution of 1789 or the October 1917 Revolution. But, in contrast to its predecessors, it has not drawn the world or even a portion of the world into its wake. It developed within China's borders, which alone, to be sure, are equivalent to a continent. It has brought great changes to economic and social organization, but the most important of them—the rural people's communes—lasted no more than a quarter of a century. And the concern for social justice, so predominant in the regime's first years, has given place to the wish to increase productivity through competition. So, taking account of the differences in international context and technological environment, can the 1949 revolution be considered to represent any more than the beginnings of a dynastic cycle pregnant with enormous reforms and hopes? And once the founding emperors have left the stage, might it not lead on to the reestablishment of the normal course of things? . . .

Despite the many areas of convergence which contemporary science and technology impose on the political and socio-economic systems they rule, modernity cannot be conceived simply as the elimination of tradition. Change can operate only by taking account of the pre-existing order, by combining with it, by partly taking it over. Modernity does not mean uniformity and, in accordance with the diversity of the field where it is realized, one must notice that it takes various forms, yielding a broad space to cultural and regional specificities. The power of a tradition also affects that of a transformation, as shown by Japan and other countries in East Asia. As for China, it remains to be seen. And one may wonder if, once realized, socialism with Chinese characteristics will be very different from capitalism with Confucian characteristics.

55

LEARNING IS NOT FOOD ON THE TABLE

LEE FEIGON

Many Western academics commented on developments among students and on the student movements of the 1980s. The great majority supported the aims of the 1989 movement, and condemned the Chinese government for its action in suppressing the students.

Lee Feigon, a scholar who has written widely on modern China and the history of the Chinese Communist Party, was among those Americans who witnessed first-hand the student movement in Beijing in the spring of 1989, living on the campus of the People's University there. He knew several of the students who played key leadership roles in the movement, and his book China Rising, *which describes in detail the student 'rising' and its unhappy suppression at the 'Tiananmen Massacre', was correspondingly influential.*

In the following passage he discusses the conditions of Chinese students and intellectuals in the period leading up to the 1989 movement. The bleak view presented here contrasts with that offered by Eric Gordon (through his wife Marie) on the eve of the Cultural Revolution in the mid-1960s.

S tudents were frustrated by their own deteriorating living and working conditions.

This was a long-standing student problem. During the dynastic period, distraught students with little hope of passing their examinations after years of study felt indignant when they were forced to occupy dirty, excrement-ridden lodging and examination booths as they crowded into the cities for their periodic tests. Similar problems have haunted China in more modern times. Concerns about lack of opportunity and resentment over inadequate, cramped living and working conditions also helped set off students in 1905, in the May Fourth era [1919], and during the Cultural Revolution.

In 1989 the same problems recurred. Chinese educators had received few personal benefits from the rapid economic progress of the 1980s. By the latter part of the decade, university professors, once the most esteemed and highly paid group in China, received less than taxi drivers or some independent produce merchants. With an annual inflation rate of 20 to 30 per cent, professors' salaries were barely adequate to provide food and clothing for their families. By 1987, spending on institutional frills was twice as high as all official expenditure on education. A 1988 survey found that the average college graduate earned about $9 per month less than those who had not gone to college. It also determined that intellectuals had less leisure time than other urban residents, contemplated an average life span of just fifty-eight years (ten years under the national average), and earned lower wages than common factory workers.

For students the situation was particularly bleak—worse, in many cases, than it had been for their rebellious colleagues earlier in this century. Chinese students were assigned to various university departments on the basis of standardized exams. Later these same students were often forced to accept jobs in small towns or in the countryside under dismal conditions and at poor salaries, a sorry fate for those who considered themselves among the best and brightest of their society. They were incensed that corrupt, know-nothing officials lived a life of leisure while they existed in squalor. The number of undergraduates leaving school rose 45 per cent in 1988, and the number who went on to graduate school fell 75 per cent.

The student plight attracted national attention early in 1989 when a college student advertised for a wife in a small paper in south central China. A young woman reader wrote to say that no one would want to marry him, but if someone did, he should try to make sure that his children did not continue on in school. 'Five years of elementary school is enough; everyone nowadays uses computers,' she argued. The position of intellectuals in China, the woman continued, was lower than that of beggars. 'Learning is not food on the table.' Although a number of readers wrote to defend the student, many also wrote to express agreement with this scathing denunciation of intellectuals.

56

MEETING VIOLENCE WITH VIOLENCE
JANE MACARTNEY

The following extract recounts how students and others felt just after the suppression of the 1989 movement and gives a good idea of how opinion changed. The Zhao referred to below is Zhao Ziyang, General Secretary of the Party at the time of the crushing of the student movement. He lost the power struggle which accompanied the crisis and was replaced by Jiang Zemin on 24 June 1989.

The author of this passage, Jane Macartney, graduated from Durham University in sinology in 1979, then worked in Taiwan, Hong Kong, and Beijing for United Press International and several business publications. In April 1989 she went back to China to cover the student demonstrations for Hong Kong-based Asiaweek *magazine. The passage comes from* The Broken Mirror: China After Tiananmen, *edited by George Hicks.*

I n defeat, the students have learned much, including the nature of their government. The storming of Beijing on June 4 enraged and alienated a generation of China's brightest and best, not just in the capital but across the country. It outraged the people of Beijing. Sympathy for the students' peaceful protest and anger at the brutality of the government's response have sparked silent, sullen disillusion up to the very highest levels of the Party and bureaucracy. Sporadic instances of campus defiance have hinted at the hatred and anger simmering beneath the surface. The students are awaiting any sign of weakness on the part of the government to raise again their dissenting voices. To prevent that, the authorities have cranked up their propaganda machinery to spread 'The Big Lie.' They have failed to address one of the fundamental problems behind the protest—the lack of an ideology. The materialism of the 'economic reforms' and the 'open-door' policies are not goals to mobilize young students hungry for ideals to the government's side. Zhao's failure to fill the ideology vacuum was one of his biggest mistakes. His successors have tumbled into the same trap: They are trying to govern a disaffected youth for whom they have replaced Marx with that powerful Chinese divinity, the God of Wealth. With reform in retreat, that goal too may be beyond the grasp of China's youth. Their despair will erupt, and next time, remembering the tragedy of their last, peaceful approach, they may meet violence with violence.

PART XIII

THE NEW DRAGONS

After a period of tension following the crisis of mid-1989, Deng Xiaoping took action early in 1992 to reinvigorate the reform policies. The result was that the economy burgeoned throughout the 1990s. Deng had formally retired just after the crisis but retained a good deal of authority until well into the 1990s; he died early in 1997 at the age of ninety-two. Jiang Zemin had assumed the position of CCP General Secretary in 1989 and retained it throughout the 1990s, strengthening his confidence and authority with the passage of time.

The effects of the 1989 crackdown on the student movement continued to be felt in the West throughout the 1990s, although with diminishing intensity as the decade progressed. Western governments placed a far higher priority on human rights in their relations with China than they had done before the 1989 crisis, but they still saw the need to deal with China. They were generally impressed with China's economic performance. Not surprisingly, they were forced to face the dilemma of whether to allow human rights issues to interfere with trade and economic relations.

57

THE NEW DRAGONS

HARRISON E. SALISBURY

To some, the 1989 crisis appeared to justify the view that the communists were a new form of imperial bureaucracy and that Mao Zedong and Deng Xiaoping, the two supreme leaders, were therefore latter-day Chinese emperors. According to this theory, democracy was irrelevant for China, because it was so alien to tradition.

One of those to liken Mao and Deng to emperors was Harrison Salisbury. His book The New Emperors *is a detailed history of the People's Republic of China up to 1992. It focuses on the two main Chinese leaders of the PRC to that time, Mao Zedong and Deng Xiaoping, and Salisbury's overall viewpoint about the impact of the past on the present is evident in the following passage.*

Hundreds of men have borne the title of emperor, *huang-ti* [*huangdi*], in China's long history. Few have exercised more power, personal and political, than Mao Zedong and Deng Xiaoping, true *huang-ti*.

The first *huang-ti* was the Yellow Emperor, the legendary ruler who founded China on the rich loess floodplains of the Yellow River. Mao led his Red armies, with Deng at his side, out of these plains to found his New China at Tiananmen in 1949.

The concept of emperor in China is intimately associated with that of the dragon. China's dragons, guardians of the throne, are unlike those of the West. They are benign and protective but can turn like terrible emperors on the people. If they do so, it is the fault of the people, not the dragons. They breathe fire and thrash their tail only if betrayed, a convenient concept for an emperor.

In Chinese custom, dynasties and bloodlines are not so important as power. The great Chinese dynastic scholar Zhang Zhi says of Mao, 'He founded the first peasant dynasty in six hundred years.' In Chinese history a capable minister or victorious general has often won the Mandate of Heaven. Deng Xiaoping fit the concept perfectly. Both men earned the title of *huang-ti* despite the fact that both considered themselves Marxists. Both were Sons of Heaven, rulers by a kind of divine right.

In the words of the preeminent scholar Derk Bodde: 'In China more perhaps than in any other country a knowledge of the past is essential for an understanding of the present.'

58

THE PARTY ON THE PRECIPICE

JIM ROHWER

Notwithstanding such a view as Salisbury's, nobody would doubt the importance of the Chinese Communist Party in the PRC's political structure. At the time of the 1989 crisis, some thought it would be shortly overthrown. For instance, in an article appearing in The New York Review of Books *on 12 October 1989, Pierre Ryckmans (Simon Leys) declared that 'the collapse of the present government is ineluctable' and that its poison had been so great, including four decades of 'relentless political terror', that 'worse horrors may follow' the overthrow.[1]*

As the 1990s wore on and the CCP showed no signs either of bowing out or of being overthrown, commentators adopted a less hostile view. The following piece by the American journalist Jim Rohwer paints a picture of a nasty but highly effective organization, one that has mellowed since 1980. This view retains something of the parallel with the past, which Salisbury emphasizes, and also some doubt as to whether the CCP can survive in power. The excerpt was published in the mid-1990s, shortly before Deng Xiaoping died.

As Deng Xiaoping grew more and more frail in the autumn of 1994 and the spring of 1995, observers of China and people who make money there became more and more exercised by the question of how the succession at the top of the Communist party would play out. They need not have lost so much sleep over it. The more serious issue for China's stability and future growth is not who triumphs in the power games at the top of the party but instead how strong its institutions are down below.

One of the best accounts of how China's Communist party works is a paper written by Yan Huai, a one-time official in the party's organization department who went into exile after the Tiananmen

Square crackdown in 1989. Mr Yan describes an organization in which the contest for supreme power is a cruel affair, conspiratorial and paranoid. It is also tempestuous and unstable, with unpredictable changes in both political atmosphere and personnel. Deng himself was disgraced and then clawed his way back into power three times. Mr Yan calculated that in the years 1949–92, on average half of the members of each Politburo Standing Committee (the highest party body) were deposed. When the changes happen, they come like a thunderclap. Then, just as swiftly, it is back to business as usual for the party apparatus.

The party has been able to recover quickly from any leadership turmoil because it has been so effective at extending its tentacles into every part of Chinese life and at rewarding its agents in the party itself, in the government, and in the army. At the end of 1994 the party had 55 million members; it is testimony to the party's continued clout (if only in delivering perks to its members) that it gained a net two million members in each of the previous two years. The party exercises control through a highly centralized and intrusive system of supervision that extends from Beijing to the smallest and most remote townships, that penetrates the organs of party and government, barracks and factories, and schools and neighbourhoods. The party, says Mr Yan, is 'an omnipresent, omniscient, crisscrossed, interwoven force controlling the entire system of political organization.'

The loyalty of government employees is assured not just by the party's watchful eye but also by a centralized system of ranking, privileges, and controls that closely follows—indeed improves upon—the two-thousand-year-old methods of the Chinese imperial bureaucracy. Even religious orders have been absorbed: 'The Buddhist abbot is ranked at the department level and the Buddhist monk is ranked at the section level.' The loyalty of army officers (who in any event have been trained for generations to obey the party's dictates) and of their men is further guaranteed by material benefits and growing military budgets. The loyalty of ordinary citizens is not needed. Only their obedience is, and the party still deploys ample measures of police-state force to secure that.

Although more of this elaborate system of control undoubtedly remains intact than outsiders can readily credit, it is also true that fifteen years of reform have substantially softened its totalitarian rigour. In many ways this is, of course, a welcome advance not only because it has already widened the scope of personal freedom in China but also because it points to a more pluralist political life in the future. As Mr Yan points out, the normal progression for a revolutionary regime confronted by political opponents is to move from shooting them to jailing them to exiling them to tolerating them; and it is not too much to expect of China that the phase of tolerance will be reached in the next ten years. Even so, the loosening of totalitarian control has had its bad side; the government's inability . . . to enforce discipline not on people at large but on its own agents. Will the party be able to re-learn this art in a more modern form?

59

THE PLAGUE OF CORRUPTION

JAMES MILES

The serious problem of corruption was one of the issues leading to the student demonstrations of 1989, yet despite official attempts to curb it, corruption continued to plague China in the 1990s. A writer who emphasizes this evil is James Miles in his book The Legacy of Tiananmen. *Graduating from Oxford in Chinese studies in 1984, Miles spent much of the fifteen years which followed as a journalist reporting about China. At the time this book was published he was Hong Kong Correspondent for the British Broadcasting Corporation (BBC) World Service.*

Corruption of course is a problem common to many countries, including industrialized nations, but in few is the problem as threatening to social and political stability as it is in China. Corruption is at least as rampant in the Indian bureaucracy, for example, as it is in China's. Yet India has mechanisms whereby the general public can vent their anger, ranging from the ballot box to their frequently exercised right to stage public demonstrations. In China, ordinary citizens can only bottle up their frustrations. When they do find a rare opportunity to air their grievances, as they did in 1989, the outpouring of rage is all the more likely to be politically destructive.

Speaking to top party leaders just a few days after the crushing of the Tiananmen Square protests, Deng [Xiaoping] decreed that between 10 and 20 'major cases' of corruption should be publicly exposed 'without delay' in order to 'satisfy the people.' Deng warned that failure to curb corruption could jeopardize attainment of the party's 'strategic goals,' But although in response to Deng's urgings the party declared its renewed determination to crack down, the problem refused to go away, not least because it affected so many people at every level of the government. In late July 1989, the Politburo announced new anti-nepotism regulations banning the children and spouses of senior leaders from working in commercial enterprises. This was aimed at the many relatives of top officials who were taking advantage of their powerful connections to make huge profits in the business world. But the new measures were halfhearted at best, applying only to relatives of officials in the Politburo, Party Secretariat, and the State Council's Executive Committee. The relatives of retired revolutionaries—the real leaders of China—were not mentioned. Thus Deng's second son, Deng Zhifang, was able to keep his job as a senior executive in the China International Trust and Investment Corporation. . . .

Deng's plan to expose 10 or 20 'major cases' of corruption ran into difficulties. There was no doubt the party could come up with many times that number of 'major cases' if it really put its mind to it. But the task of exposing corruption inevitably became bogged down in factional politics. Hard-liners pursued corrupt reformers with greater vigour than they did members of their own ranks. . . .

Many ordinary Chinese complain that corruption was more the rule than the exception. Taxi drivers moan about police routinely extorting money or cigarettes as 'fines' for nonexistent traffic violations. A friend of mine in the police force told me that even a murderer could be freed from jail on payment of the right bribe. He himself managed to secure the release of a relative suspected of political crimes by bribing his relative's guards. To get a telephone or a better apartment, admission to a good school for one's children or decent medical treatment more often than not requires handouts of cash or gifts to the right officials. Foreign businesspeople often complain about increasingly blatant demands by their Chinese partners for gifts, overseas trips, or even the sponsorship of education abroad for their children. The foreign tourist might see little if any sign of such corruption, but any foreign resident in China knows how important it is to provide at least cigarettes and imported soft drinks or alcohol for the plumber or electrician to make sure the job is done well and promptly.

Less visible but far more serious corruption is rife in the higher ranks of the bureaucracy, among those who have access to or control over coveted resources such as building materials, coal, oil, steel, fertilizer, or means of transport. The gradual freeing of prices in recent years has helped reduce attempts to cash in on the difference between fixed and market prices, but profiteering remains rampant.

60

THE IMPROVED HUMAN CONDITION

MICHEL OKSENBERG, MICHAEL SWAINE, AND DANIEL LYNCH

The following extract summarizes one view on the human rights problem, which weighed so heavily in relations between China and Western countries in the 1990s. This view has gained widespread acceptance in the United States and elsewhere.

The authors—Michael Oksenberg, Michael Swaine, and Daniel Lynch— are all American academics, the first two senior specialists on contemporary China. They formed part of a larger study group sponsored by the Pacific Council on International Policy, which seeks to help leaders from many sectors respond to a rapidly changing world, and the RAND Center for Asia-Pacific Policy, a non-partisan multidisciplinary research centre.

The horrors of June, 1989—when the leaders ordered the People's Liberation Army (PLA) to occupy Tiananmen Square by force—remain indelibly imprinted in the minds of many Americans, for whom the brave soul who defied the column of invading tanks captured the moment of a regime crushing its own people. With that searing image still so fresh, many Americans are naturally inclined to believe the worst about the Chinese regime and its treatment of the Chinese people.

Yet the fact is that since that tragic moment, the human condition of most Chinese has continued to improve, as it had done from the end of the Mao era in 1976 until 1989. And we are not just speaking about improvements in per capita income and the availability of consumer goods. China's leaders have undertaken a number of measures to expand the political rights of citizens:

- They are attempting to introduce the rule of law. The leaders have instructed local governments to inform the populace about the laws that the national government has enacted and that local agencies are responsible for implementing. When local agencies disregard, exceed, or violate these laws, citizens in some locales are now able to request the local court to annul the action. Lawyers are being trained in modest numbers and law offices are being established to assist plaintiffs to bring suits against the state. However, the courts do not have the right of judicial review to examine whether laws and administrative regulations are in compliance with the constitution. And introduction of the rule of law will be hampered by the wide administrative discretion that local officials enjoy and the dependence of the courts on these officials for funding and personnel appointments.

- Village elections have been introduced and monitored to enable villagers to participate in the selection of their leaders. Many non-communists have been elected. To be sure, the electoral process in most areas remains firmly under the control of the communist Party, and the village Party organization still plays a major role in running village affairs. But the idea of democracy is being introduced at the grass-roots level.
- Citizens have the right temporarily to migrate without first securing permission of their superiors. Peasants can lease out land that the village has assigned to them and that they choose not to farm themselves.
- The populace clearly enjoys a wider range of choice in the cultural domain. The number of magazines, newspapers, and books being published is increasing dramatically. Even in rural areas, video cassettes of Hong Kong and Taiwan movies, contemporary and classical foreign novels in translation, and traditional Chinese novels are widely available.

Arguably, most Chinese enjoy a greater degree of freedom than at any time in the past century. And yet most Americans would find the human rights situation in China intolerable. Freedom of speech and assembly do not exist. The government's treatment of Tibetan Buddhism is undoubtedly oppressive. Torture, arbitrary arrest, and indiscriminate application of the death penalty are widespread. The state interferes in the most cherished moments of life's passages—birth, marriage, and death, dictating the number of children a couple may have, the age of marriage, and burial practices. High-level officials whom the government-controlled media have identified as guilty of corruption go untried in court, their misdeeds not clearly explained to the public, while lower-level officials convicted of seemingly lesser crimes are sentenced to death. Although in private Chinese are quite willing to express their political views to close friends or foreigners whose discretion they trust, individuals who publish views or undertake actions that oppose the regime or denigrate specific leaders are arrested. The regime does not tolerate organized political dissent.

In short, although China's human rights record is improving, it still is unsatisfactory by most standards, including those held by most Chinese. To improve the human condition and to create a social setting that will truly sustain a regime committed to human rights require the strengthening of such norms as respect for the rule of law, trust in and a sense of obligation toward people outside one's own circle of family and friends, and tolerance of diversity. These will take many years, perhaps decades, to inculcate.

61

PROSPEROUS FREEDOM

GEOFFREY MURRAY

As the 1990s progressed, China continued to flourish economically, even after the late 1990s economic crisis struck Indonesia, Japan, and other countries of East and South-East Asia. At the same time, however, China refused to change its political system and persisted in clamping down on dissenting political activists. Many in the West were not only impressed with China's economic prosperity but praised China's political direction.

The following example of this view of China takes issue with the condemnatory attitude towards China. It is written by Geoffrey Murray, a Western journalist turned scholar and business and media training consultant, who lived in Vietnam, Japan, Singapore, and China from 1966 onward.

Walk down any street in Shanghai or Beijing today and you stare into the face of China's future: young people wearing name-brand clothes, armed with cellular phones and pagers. Stop a few on the street and ask them what freedom is and they are more likely to point to their bulging wallets than to politics. I often read laments by American journalists and writers about the perceived political apathy among China's younger generation, which they somehow see as a disturbing trend. Where, they ask in anguish, are the democracy activists who were so prominent in 1989, seeking to loosen the Communist Party's grip on politics and society? Well, some at least are now more intent on making money than disturbing the political *status quo.* The most prominent leader of the 1989 movement in Tiananmen Square, who emotionally assured the world she was willing to die for her beliefs, is now living comfortably in the United States studying for her MBA.

For most young Chinese, superficially at least, freedom is narrowly defined as economic success and the ability to spend money on things that have long been available to Westerners—fast food, the latest fashions, and new technological products, as well as club-hopping and rock 'n' roll. Of course, one aspect of freedom is the ability to eat, dress, and live as one pleases. There was little room for individual preferences or consumerism in Mao's more restrictive era, when Versace jeans or an air-conditioned apartment would have been condemned as 'bourgeois' and anti-Communist. The progress made under Deng Xiaoping in these areas has been widely documented. But today's young Chinese do not seem to mind that there have been no similar reforms regarding the other side of freedom: political freedom, including the right to choose one's leaders and express one's thought and opinions freely.

And, while this may not be something for Western political analysts to lament, I find it hard to blame young Chinese for wanting to get away from the obsession with politics that ruined the lives of their parents. At the same time, while quite happy to buy Western products, many young Chinese are now more ready to join their government in criticizing the West for its hypocrisy and double standards, even if they may not have a clear understanding of what they are criticizing.

A typical comment, usually by people who have never been to the United States, for example, is to condemn Americans as bossy, simple-minded, and too critical of a country that they have little understanding of. 'They're simply scared that China is becoming too powerful,' they say, referring to Washington's penchant for criticizing China's politics and human rights.

62

OF RICHES AND VILLAGES

SHERYL WUDUNN

In the 1980s and 1990s, the West generally viewed China's economy very positively. The following article is by a third-generation Chinese-American from New York, Sheryl WuDunn, who was a correspondent for The New York Times in Beijing in the late 1980s and early 1990s. Her husband, Nicholas D. Kristof, whom she married in 1988, became the bureau chief of The New York Times the same year in Beijing, remaining in the post for nearly five years.

Daqiuzhuang, China—Yang Yanru, a middle-aged woman who keeps her 11-room house spotless, could have been standing on a typical street in an affluent American suburb, bidding her guests goodbye after a luncheon.

Except for her crooked teeth, and a collar that suggested her man-tailored shirt was made in the 1960s, there was little to suggest that Ms Yang was once a peasant who got her eggs from the chicken coop in the backyard. Now she is one of China's new rich, a woman who says she doesn't have to hold down a job because her husband makes so much money. She can spend her afternoons entertaining visitors, she said, or playing mah-jongg with friends.

About 45 miles down a narrow, bumpy road from the heart of Tianjin city, Daqiuzhuang has earned a reputation as a village that got rich through a strange blend of Communism and capitalism.

Factories here operate 24 hours a day, seven days a week, paying salaries of $800 to $900 a year to most village residents. Most of the rest of the money is plowed back into businesses or is spent on communal projects or perks for bosses and model workers.

'Even in my dreams, I never thought life could be so good,' said Ms Yang, who knits when she is not watching one of her three color televisions or talking on one of her two telephones.

This village of 4,400 people has 13 Mercedes Benzes and nearly 140 other imported luxury cars. In 1990, Daqiuzhuang's per capita income was $3,400, ten times China's national average; last year, officials say, it soared even higher, to an estimated $8,400.

The village runs the factories that make the money—226 enterprises in all. Factory managers receive a share of profits in addition to their salaries, and their incomes can be enormous. In 1990, the last year for which figures are fully calculated, Ms Yang's husband, who manages a construction business, was entitled to $9,300, though she said he took only a part of that and returned the rest to the enterprise.

No Daqiuzhuang citizen pays a cent for housing, electricity, hot water, gas, medical care or the 11 years of education to which every child is entitled. The village also invests about $3.7 million a year in building houses and apartment buildings for its 1,300 families. If an employee is rewarded as a model worker, as Ms Yang's husband was, he receives one of 300 furnished, nicely painted two-story brick houses.

'Here we have reached the perfect form of socialism: Communism,' said Sun Guiqiu, a senior official in the village.

But capitalism seems to be the major factor in the village's business success. Factories keep careful track of costs, pay their employees by the piece rate, and use complex systems of incentives to increase production.[1] . . .

63
AN EDUCATIVE JUMP

STANLEY ROSEN

China's increasing prosperity and privatization brought problems, some of them serious. In education, one result was school dropouts. The following passage considers the reasons why this happened in the countryside in the 1990s.

The author is Stanley Rosen, a specialist on contemporary China who has written extensively on social and political change in China, the history of the People's Republic of China (PRC), and the Cultural Revolution. The passage comes from his chapter 'Education and Economic Reform' in The China Handbook, *edited by Christopher Hudson.*

Many studies, particularly in rural areas, have attempted to determine the reasons for leaving school. Researchers consistently have found that economic reforms play a major role in school dropouts. The increased cost of education, including both school fees and student expenses, have made schooling unaffordable for many families. Rising tuition costs are the result of increasing fees imposed on schools. . . . Student expenses such as textbooks and school supplies also have risen sharply, making it difficult for peasant families to afford to keep a child in school.

While fees and expenditures for education clearly are the leading reason that dropout rates have increased, other factors related to economic reform either directly or indirectly play a role. First, the new policy of charging tuition . . . at the university level has begun to have an impact, particularly on rural households. Already compelled to pay close to 1,000 *yuan* [about US$125] to send a child to high school, families dependent on agriculture recognize early on that they cannot afford the minimum 1,000 *yuan* of yearly college tuition. Second, the reform of the state's personnel system, under which college and specialized secondary school graduates are no longer guaranteed job allocations, has served to lessen the attraction of higher education for peasant families. Previously, the main attraction of schooling for rural families was the possibility that their children would be able to 'leap over the village gate' and leave farming altogether. Now that graduates are expected to find their own jobs, parents fear that even if their children pass the matriculation examination, enter a college, and pay the required tuition fees, poor employment prospects may lurk at the end of the process. For many families the risk is unacceptable given a cost-benefit analysis and the other options available to them. Many students choose instead to 'jump into the sea' (i.e., engage in business). Examples of dropouts who have succeeded in business are legion and, unlike the past when entrepreneurs were suspected of 'capitalist tendencies,' such people today elicit awe and admiration.

PART XIV

SOCIAL MALAISE

China's increasing economic prosperity and political influence since 1992 has had a profound effect on Chinese society. The lifestyle of the average Chinese, especially in the cities, has become much more varied and interesting. But at the same time, the control that the authorities exercise over the country has continued to disintegrate. Hardly anyone still believes in Marxism and in 'serving the people', ideas which would now appear ridiculous to most people, especially the young. Many are worried that the one-child policy is breeding a selfish and spoiled generation of people who have become used to being treated as 'little emperors' and 'little princesses'. Crime rates have continued to rise and, for the first time since the Chinese Communist Party (CCP) came into power, narcotics have become a serious problem.

The divide between urban and rural areas has always been enormous in China. Since the 1990s, however, it has become bigger than ever, at least in social terms. The countryside has seen the revival of many traditional patterns, some of them extremely negative, especially those concerning the status of women. In the cities, on the other hand, society has become astonishingly modern: the standard of living has risen spectacularly while unemployment has increased dramatically; old certainties have slackened; there is greater freedom but, conversely, less security.

64

THE MODERN WOMAN'S LOT

SHERYL WUDUNN

The position of women, a matter of major concern in Western countries over the past decades, was also a frequent topic of reporting on China. This was especially the case with the controversial one-child policy, a policy closely related to women's issues.

In the following passage Sheryl WuDunn discusses the position of women in China, the improvements under Mao Zedong, and the new situation under Deng Xiaoping in the 1980s and 1990s. Her mixed impressions show disappointment and totally lack the enthusiasm displayed in her comments on the rich Chinese village of Daqiuzhuang, recorded in Chapter 62. But it is striking that the central figure of the Chinese village returns to the story. The passage comes from the book China Wakes, The Struggle for the Soul of a Rising Power, *which WuDunn wrote jointly with her husband Nicholas D. Kristof.*

One day in late summer a thirty-year-old woman, slightly frail and innocent-looking, was sitting on a hillside near the grain fields of Liaohepo Village in Henan Province. Zuo Dechang, a young hoodlum who had been in and out of the local police station for various crimes, spotted her and cozied up to her. She wasn't much for conversation, for she was mentally retarded, but Zuo didn't mind. He brought her back to his village and tried to find a man who might buy her as a wife.

'I have no money,' an unmarried peasant told Zuo, as the two negotiated a deal. 'But I have a small calf. What would you think if I gave you this calf in exchange for this woman you've brought to our village?'

Well, Zuo thought, I could sell the calf for a bit of money. 'It's a deal,' he told the farmer, and the woman changed hands.

Her new husband gave her hardly anything to eat and little clothing to protect herself against the cold. A few months later, on a wintry day in 1990, she died.

A woman for a calf.

Something, I decided, was wrong with the picture of Communist equality that I had initially absorbed. When I first arrived in China, I was impressed that almost every woman I met had an occupation or a career. I did not notice any discrimination against women, and I met intelligent and capable women in academia, business, and journalism, as well as gutsy female vegetable merchants, engineering consultants, and toy makers. When we got to the Chinese border on Macao during my first trip into China in 1987, a crowd of ambitious, pushy cabdrivers crowded around Nick and me in pursuit of our fare. The most reasonable price was quoted to us by the most levelheaded of them all, a twenty-seven-year-old woman who owned her own taxi, and we chose her.

I thought, This is equality! I felt better about China itself, for as a Chinese woman, I was troubled greatly by the traditional distaste and discrimination that women faced. It was fine to be proud of the Great Wall but not of a 4,000-year legacy of abandoning female babies, of binding girls' feet, of keeping girls illiterate. Until the turn of the century, many Chinese girls were not even given names: They were called Eldest Daughter, Second Daughter, and so on, until they married and took on a combination of their fathers' and husbands' surnames. . . .

I felt the weight of tradition in part because my own grandmother had had her feet bound as a young girl. This was an excruciating process, typically begun when a child was five to ten years old. Long strips of cloth were tightened around a girl's feet and maintained until the late teens. The binding forced the bones to break and the skin to rot. Toes sometimes dropped off, pus and blood covered the wounds, and the smell was sometimes overpowering. When Grandma moved to Canada with my grandfather in the 1920s, she unbound her feet, but it was too late: They had turned into flat, stubby blocks.

Mao tried to end all that. Foot binding itself had pretty much died out by 1949, but the Communists pressed relentlessly to admit women into the ranks of human beings. One of the Communist Party's greatest achievements—and one for which it is not given adequate credit—is its elevation of the status of Chinese women. . . .

The party encouraged women to join its ranks, to become officials, to run factories, to do things they had never done before. The number of women in the industrial labour force soared, from 600,000 in 1949 to more than 50 million today, so that now some 82 per cent of working-age women in the cities hold jobs. These gains gave women some economic independence and self-confidence. Side by side with their husbands, they built huts and tilled the fields. Above all, the party oversaw a revolution in educational practices, mobilizing peasant girls to go to school. For the first time in Chinese history, large numbers of peasant women graduated from the status of donkeys, they became almost human beings and not just walking wombs. . . .

So when I arrived in China, I was generally impressed by the status of women. And with the new opportunities generated by a market economy, I expected life for women to get even better.

Then one day, I met Yang Yanru, a middle-aged peasant near Tianjin whose husband had become rich doing business. He asked her to stop working, and she was happy just to stay at home tidying up the house. That nagged at me. I could understand that now that she was rich she had better things to do with her time than to slave away in a factory for measly pay. But the same thing was happening all over China, and it seemed funny to me that economic progress in China would mean more housewives and fewer career women. What ever happened to Mao's belief in equality?

As I talked to more women and got better acquainted with their status, it became clear that the problems ran far deeper. The obstacle was not just the strength of traditional beliefs but the invisible hand of the market itself. The market economy raised living standards for women along with men, but it also led to the return of the male-dominated Chinese society—coupled with the sexist features of Western society. Advertisers quickly discovered that the best way to market their products was by airing commercials showing lovely young women, preferably wearing as little as possible. To promote sales of weapons abroad, the army began publishing a calendar with a pinup each month of a buxom young woman clutching a gun. In the 1994 calendar, for example, Miss February wears a bikini top and a red skirt slit to the waist, accompanied by an AK-47 assault rifle. Miss November wears a strapless formal, high heels, red gloves—and carries a sub machine gun in her right hand.

Nick once visited a school in Tianjin and was shown a twenty-minute introductory video that the principal had prepared. It began with a five-minute scene of the newly arrived high school girls scrubbing themselves from head to toe in the shower. The principal seemed to think that this was a tribute to his open-mindedness. Likewise, pornography and prostitution spread rapidly throughout China beginning in the 1980s, and bosses began to hire pretty young women as ornaments or playthings.

'These days if you're a woman, you're as good as a commodity,' said Lihong, a young Chinese businesswoman whose work in a joint venture brings her in contact with men and women of many ranks and backgrounds. . . .

65

FEMALE CHATTEL

SETH FAISON

The Fourth United Nations World Conference on Women, held in Beijing in September 1995, became a centrepiece event, giving rise to much commentary on the status of women in China. The following dispatch by Seth Faison, a journalist working for The New York Times, *covers the conference and its context. Xian, capital of Shaanxi Province, is a major city south-west of Beijing.*

Xian, China—In the shadow of the ancient wall that still surrounds this city, several hundred people gather each day along a muddy street to offer themselves to employers at an unofficial labour market.

Many are young women from the countryside, and for them the market holds a special danger: it may be the first stop on a journey that begins with the promise of a job, sees rape and violent beatings along the way, and ends in a life of domestic slavery.

Countless women have been kidnapped from this market in Xian, from similar markets in other cities, and from bus stops and train stations in towns all over China. Typically, a woman is lured into the custody of one or more criminal middlemen, beaten into submission, and delivered to a stranger who will call her his wife.

The Chinese call it 'the abducting and selling of women.' The practice, mixing an age-old disregard for the rights of women with a modern passion for profit, seems to be rising at an alarming rate, Chinese advocates of women's rights and official Chinese newspapers say.

The causes are many. Young women are more and more eager to venture outside the safety of a home village; unmarried farmers can increasingly afford the $250 to $500 that it costs to buy them; middlemen more easily roam from city to country to conduct their business.

At the Fourth World Conference on Women, Chinese officials are expected to join a chorus of calls for better protection of the rights of women. Yet when it comes to the selling of women, the authorities show a tragic indifference to what women's rights advocates now consider the most pernicious violation of human rights in their nation.

'This is the most horrific problem facing women in China today,' said Wang Xingjuan, president of the Women's Research Institute at the Chinese Academy of Management Science in Beijing. 'We have to do more to stop it.'

Although statistics are incomplete and many cases go unreported, women's advocates say that at least tens of thousands of women are now sold into slavery in China each year.

Many escape, but many more, ashamed to return to their families, are believed to eventually accept their predicament.[1]

66

AN UNACKNOWLEDGED LIBERATION

LAURENCE BRAHM

*A somewhat more positive view on women in China can be found in a
1996 book by Laurence Brahm, an investment advisor and author. Brahm
is more concerned with economics and politics than society, but his book
does include a chapter on 'Humanism'.*

The World Conference on Women

The World Conference on Women held in Beijing in 1995
brought with it a few questions for the West. Delegates went
to China ready to make the point that Western women had
been liberated and that they had something to teach their
communist sisters in China. It was a big surprise for more than a
few to realize that China is the equal of Western nations on this
issue—this is even more remarkable considering that China's
feudal traditions (foot binding and concubinage) continued into
the first half of this century.

While Western women may be more liberated in the sense of
sexual equality, and the degree of free sex that is acceptable in
Western society is still somewhat discouraged in China, no one at
the Conference was in a position to criticize the advances made by
women in Chinese society, in both the business and political
spheres.

The equality of women

Currently, some 46 per cent of China's workforce is comprised of
women. Women hold executive positions in many corporations in
China, both private and State-owned. Women in China hold senior
government positions, a fact which Chinese take pride in. For
instance, in less than a decade, two women, first Chen Muhua and

most recently Wu Yi, have held the position of Minister of Foreign Trade and Economic Cooperation, one of China's most powerful ministries under the State Council. There were 626 women deputies in the Eighth National People's Congress, China's parliament.

In short, Article 48 of the first Constitution of the People's Republic of China gave women equality. The Equal Rights Amendment, granting women equality with men under the American Constitution, has never been passed by Congress.

In most Chinese households, both men and women work. Both in turn are responsible for taking care of the children, picking them up from school and dropping them off. Other activities are shared, such as cooking. I have never met a Chinese male who was not capable of cooking—and who was not totally unabashed by the fact he cooked for his family. Often the grandparents live with the parents, or close by, as is the tradition in Chinese society. This is beneficial, as they are available to take care of the children, and this in turn gives some purpose to their own lives. It also leads to a better family-oriented environment for bringing up children, thereby avoiding some of the social problems seen in the West.

The one-child policy

The American delegates went to the Women's Conference prepared to point out that among the peasant population of rural China there are instances where girls are sold or given away in preference to male children. They were eager to criticize China's one-child policy as being the cause of this 'human rights abuse'; others criticized the easy availability of abortion services in China as being another example of the evil of this policy.

China has a population of 1.3 billion, 25 per cent of the world's population in a land the size of the US; more than half of China's land mass is either desert or uninhabitable mountains. The coastal regions, the Yellow and Yangtze river basins, and the subtropical provinces of Guangdong, Guangxi, and Yunnan are the key rice and foodstuff-producing areas of the country.

The one-child policy is virtually the only way China can currently control its population: it has been implemented against a background of tradition which calls for large extended families, and a traditional peasant outlook in the rural areas which considers the more bodies under the household roof, the more *mu* of fields that can be ploughed and tended. The fact that this policy is being implemented successfully in order to avert what could become a food-population crisis of unimaginable proportions in the twenty-first century if not controlled through administrative methods in the twentieth, demonstrates the power of a guided market economy.

While the West has been slow to criticize India or a number of African and Latin American countries which are also having trouble coping with accelerated population growth and suffering the death tolls brought about by uncontrollable diseases and mass starvation, it is quick to label China's one-child policy as a 'human rights violation'. In fact, this policy is being implemented for the very purpose of ensuring basic human rights in China.

67

CRIME AND PROSTITUTION IN HAINAN

JOHN GITTINGS

John Gittings, quoted in Chapter 43, here comments on aspects of crime and prostitution in Hainan Island in the far south of China. Haikou is the island's capital.

Hainan was one of two provinces singled out in 1992 by the Ministry of Public Security in Beijing for an intensive anti-gun drive—the other was drug-laden Yunnan on the border with Burma. The Chinese press, in an unusually explicit account, reported the public destruction of arms and ammunition a year later. Since Hainan became a province in 1988, a police official explained, there had been a massive increase in the 'illegal manufacture, sale, and private collection of arms' and in armed crimes. During the crackdown, the police claimed to have destroyed nearly 200 'dens' where arms were made or stored, and to have arrested more than 650 'gangsters'. Unfortunately the effort had to be repeated just one year later but made little difference. In the next official figures for January—June 1994, the authorities claimed to have arrested 5,500 criminals, broken up 318 criminal gangs and discovered 525 criminal hide-outs, and captured 2,556 guns including 199 combat weapons.

Prostitution in Hainan is widespread and unchecked, and the 'lemon tea-time' at the Haikou Hotel has become a tourist attraction. Most of the women come from Guangzhou, Guangxi or Shanghai, a few from the north-east. They wear expensive white slacks, pink or yellow silk blouses and have elaborate hairstyles. Protective young men in expensive leather jackets keep a watchful eye. The 'chickens' chat among themselves or peer, looking for customers, into powder-compact mirrors. The whole café is raised on a carpeted dais in the hotel foyer: 'Chickens', clients and spectators are all together on the stage. There is a piano with a crimson cover on a green pedestal for use in the evening. Local waitresses, laughing a little, take orders for lemon tea—the signal of willingness to do business. 'The police never enter hotel rooms here,' a resident explains, 'unlike Guangzhou where they do so from time to time and levy fines by credit card. Here it is all arranged through the hotel security guards, who then pay off the police. They have become very wealthy men.'

68

THE RUBBLE OF MARXISM

CRAIG DIETRICH

The market for university and college textbooks on China has grown with the greater openness emerging since the late 1970s. One which has done well is Craig Dietrich's People's China, *a history of the PRC. First published in 1986, it went to a second edition in 1994 and a third in 1998. The following is part of the second edition's concluding summation on the situation in China in the 1990s. At the time of publication the author had taught Chinese history at the University of Southern Maine for over twenty years.*

An image of tradition and modernity in Zhouzhuang, a small town near Shanghai. The old style has been retained as closely as possible, but there are also signs of modernity in the form of electric power. Photograph by Colin Mackerras.

In regard to ideology and culture, the reform period has stirred the once-quiescent pot into a roiling soup of contradiction and confusion. Marxism and socialism are hard pressed to retain any integrity, as official ideologies attempt to refashion some of the fundamental building blocks. What, after all, does socialism mean when it must find a place for all kinds of 'capitalistic' elements? Calling it 'socialism with Chinese characteristics' helps a little, but not much. Furthermore, Marxism's decline has left a cultural vacuum. Consumption, money-making, and Hong Kong fashions cannot define a fully meaningful existence. Traditional practices and folk religion have reappeared in the villages but may also be unable to shape life in a modern context of mobility, gender demands, and international economics.

Western ideas like freedom, democracy, and individualism flourish among the educated, but not necessarily among ordinary people; because Western societies, the United States in particular, present ambiguous models, the 'streets of gold' myths clashing with news reports of drugs, crime, and chaos. Hence the intellectual and cultural challenge: how to fashion on the rubble of Marxism (and while the rulers stubbornly chant their Marxist mantras) a reasonably coherent set of values and social principles.

69

BURYING MAO

RICHARD BAUM

Professor Richard Baum of the Department of Political Science at the University of California, Los Angeles is a specialist on contemporary China. His book Burying Mao, Chinese Politics in the Age of Deng Xiaoping *offers the following passage on how he sees Chinese society on the centenary of Mao Zedong's birth (26 December 1893). It is hardly surprising that the picture is pessimistic from the point of view of Mao's aspirations for China. Baum drily comments in the book's last sentence that 'had the Chairman lived to witness his centenary, he would not have been pleased'. It is also rather a grim picture from the point of view of the reformist ideology espoused by Deng Xiaoping, let alone from a Western viewpoint.*

An increase in violent crime—70 per cent of it committed by young people under twenty-five, and much of it gang-related—was also acknowledged by the Chinese government, as was the fact that since the 1980s there had been a tenfold increase in the number of youthful criminal offenders. In 1992 alone, Chinese police reportedly confiscated 200,000 illegal firearms. Also on the rise were crimes of violence against authority. In the three years from 1990 to July 1993, over 4,700 public security personnel and local police were killed or wounded while on duty. According to China's chief government prosecutor, Liu Fuzhi, the new epidemic of crime was linked to activities of mafia-like triad gangs who were said to be on a rampage throughout the country.

Cadre corruption also continued to flourish. According to a report issued by Liu Fuzhi in July 1993, the number of government officials involved in bribery, embezzlement, and other forms of corruption was 'increasing nonstop' despite a substantial rise in the apprehension of wrongdoers. Although growing numbers of cadres faced criminal probes, relatively few were prosecuted. . . .

Corruption, speculation, and profiteering were also on the rise at the upper reaches of China's military establishment. With the PLA [People's Liberation Army] actively involved in a variety of large-scale profit-making activities (*bingshang*), there were plentiful opportunities for private commercial gain by well-connected staff officers. According to foreign intelligence estimates, extrabudgetary sources generated approximately ¥30 billion [US$4 billion] in military income in 1992—accounting for almost half of the PLA's total outlays. . . . So serious was the situation that two leading members of the MAC [Military Affairs Commission], generals Liu Huaqing and Zhang Zhen, writing in July 1993 on the eve of the sixty-sixth anniversary of the founding of the PLA, warned that the 'growing tide of corruption, money worshipping, and hedonism' in the PLA constituted a 'threat to the development of the army.'

A major epidemic of kidnapping, prostitution, and drug abuse was another source of growing concern. At the Eighth NPC [National People's Congress, in March 1993], it was conservatively reported that more than 100,000 offenders had been convicted since 1988 for crimes of inducing or forcing women into prostitution, abducting and selling women or children for gain, trafficking drugs, and producing or distributing pornographic materials. This was just the tip of a much larger iceberg, however, since the government subsequently reported that over 50,000 purveyors of pornography had been arrested in 1992 alone, along with more than 75,000 pimps and 'sex-traders.' In Guangzhou municipality there were an estimated 30,000 prostitutes working the streets, tourist hotels, and karaoke bars. In February 1993 Chinese authorities reported that they had rescued 40,000 women and 3,500 children from criminal abductors in the past two years.

The figures on drug abuse (primarily opium and heroin addiction) were equally alarming, with the number of registered addicts doubling annually, from approximately 70,000 in 1990 to over 250,000 in 1992. In 1993 Chinese drug enforcement officials acknowledged that only a small proportion of China's addicts had registered with the government. Reports from Yunnan and Guangdong suggested that the total number of drug users was probably manyfold higher than the government's official estimates. . . .

Such fragmentary data bore vivid testimony to a significantly strained social fabric. Among Chinese youths, a new crisis of faith was everywhere in evidence. Up and down the bustling, densely populated east coast of China, from Harbin to Hainan, observers noted a deepening mood of alienation and anomie among young people, large numbers of whom were increasingly turning to 'get-rich-quick' schemes, to religion, to the martial arts, or to sex, drugs, and rock 'n' roll as quick-fix antidotes to decaying belief systems, declining moral standards, and disintegrating social controls.

On the whole, the social indicators in 1993 were strikingly negative, necessitating a cautious assessment of the country's outward appearance of pro-reform dynamism and prosperity.

70

THANK GOD ALMIGHTY,
I AIN'T WHAT I WAS

NICHOLAS D. KRISTOF AND SHERYL WUDUNN

Nicholas D. Kristof and Sheryl WuDunn sum up their impressions of China at the end of their five-year stint there with The New York Times. *Despite grave reservations, the impressions are fundamentally positive and optimistic.*

D uring the American civil rights struggle, the Reverend Martin Luther King, Jr, used to tell of the prayer of an old black woman. 'Lord, I ain't what I want to be,' Dr King quoted her as saying. 'I ain't what I ought to be. But thank God

One of the chief execution grounds of the Nanjing Massacre of 1937–8, this museum was set up in the 1990s to mark the sixtieth anniversary. The large statue in the centre is a reminder of the grimness and horror of the event. Photograph by Colin Mackerras.

Almighty, I ain't what I was.' That prayer could be echoed by nearly every Chinese alive today.

We have a Chinese friend in the chemical industry who puts it a different way. Our friend, a man who grew up barefoot in the countryside, now wears a necktie and lives the good life as head of the representative office of an American company. We would occasionally drop by his office and relate the latest little tidbit we'd heard: some new sexual harassment case, a corruption scandal, a peasant rebellion, a soccer riot. And he would invariably shrug and say, 'China's a normal country now.'

His point was that most countries around the world have corruption scandals, peasant rebellions, and soccer riots. It was only in the artificial environment of Maoism, when there was no oxygen to sustain life, that such things did not happen. In the regular hurly-burly of China, there will be such upheavals: There will be village riots, labour clashes, and political demonstrations. Tear gas will waft through Beijing and Chengdu and Changchun.

Those kinds of things happen in normal countries, particularly in developing countries, but they do not mean that the system will collapse. Instead, as our friend sees it, such disturbances can even be seen as a measure of normality. We're not sure he's right, but we hope so.

PART XV

LOOKING
FORWARDS

A t the end of the twentieth century, sinophiles and sinophobes produced remarkably different assessments of both China's situation and prospects. While it was clear at the end of the twentieth century that China had risen spectacularly since the days of Mao Zedong, many doubted whether the rise would last.

One sinophobic opinion found commonly in the 1990s, especially in the United States, was that a revived China was a country to be feared. According to this argument, an increasingly modern China would threaten both its neighbours and the West. A similarly sinophobic outlook was that China would degenerate into chaos and bloodshed and the Chinese Communist Party (CCP) would be overthrown by contending groups struggling to fill the remaining power vacuum, the fate of many communist countries. Sinophiles, on the other hand, saw a risen China as something to be welcomed: as a relatively benign country on the international scene, it could be a force of stability in Asia and the rest of world.

Although nobody knows the future, speculation over China's development will continue to flourish. Whether sinophile or sinophobe, optimist or pessimist, no one can doubt that China, with its vast tradition and culture, will inevitably produce an enormous impact upon its neighbours and the world.

71

A RETURN TO THE POLICE STATE

LEE FEIGON

The crackdown on the student movement in the middle of 1989 affected views not only of the present but also of the future. The following is a typical evaluation of the situation in China and its prospects for the future just after the suppression. Its author is Lee Feigon, already quoted in Chapter 55.

The result of Deng's policy is likely to be similar to this description by Stan Sesser of what occurred in Burma after the military took over the economy in 1962: 'As they took over manufacturing and trade, they got the perks—the house, the car, gasoline, a telephone. But nine times out of ten they didn't know what they were doing. The Burmese were having enough trouble making their industry operate without having this intervening layer. Your boss was always someone from the military and he was in it for the plunder, building on Ne Win's premise that you couldn't trust the Burmese PhDs who had been educated in the West.'

In China the people who have so far suffered most from the new economic policy are those in urban areas. They are the same people who showed their disrespect for the country's rulers, and they are being punished for it. In the fall of 1989 the government announced that grain production was still well below 1985 levels despite better weather and an all-out effort, which for the first time in two years included cash payments to the peasants for what they produced. This cash was raised largely from urban workers, whose salaries were cut by as much as one-fourth. In lieu of the cash owed them, these labourers were paid with government bonds. As a result, the number of IOUs distributed to the peasants were far fewer than in the past.

While Deng and other old hard-liners have their revenge, their solution does not bode well for the long-term health of the Chinese economy. As the government cuts urban salaries it destroys worker morale and discipline, making it harder to improve the very industries Deng wants to emphasize. The simultaneous limitations placed on new industries that developed as a result of earlier reforms make a Brezhnev-style stagnation all but inevitable for China's cities. Even if the government continues to milk urban areas to help the countryside—which is unlikely unless the country's leaders are willing to tolerate a return to the industrial dark ages—in the long run agriculture is likely to suffer even more. . . .

This is unlikely to mean a return to the collectivization of the past, but it does mean a reversion to the kind of police state now being abandoned in eastern Europe. The smallest decision will be channeled to higher authorities, to be answered after an interminable delay by those with little knowledge of the actual situation. Normally cautious bureaucrats will naturally become more so. Responsible Chinese officials are likely to grow increasingly wary about contacts with countries of the West which are seen to be infecting China with the disease of democracy.

The ineptitude which the hard-liners have shown even in that area of the Chinese economy that has performed best—agriculture—may be a sign of things to come. There could well be a return to the situation that existed in China from the time of the Communist victory in 1949 until 1976, when, with the exception of only one year, 1957, per capita food consumption did not reach even the meager levels that had existed in the country before World War II.

72

CHINA WILL BE DEMOCRATIC

ANDREW NATHAN

After the 1989 student movement, democracy and the prospects for this form of government became a major issue for discussion among those concerned with China in the West. In academic circles, probably the most important writer on this matter was Andrew Nathan, an established sinologist at Columbia University who had already published widely on China's history in the Republican period and on democracy and human rights in contemporary China. In the following passage, published the year after the 1989 crisis, he puts forward an essentially optimistic view, predicting that a form of democracy will eventually be established in China.

Nathan hints here at the fear of China. This fear had been a factor in Western perceptions of China several times before, most notably in the 1950s and 1960s. In the early 1990s, there was a revival of the notion that China would soon become a threat to security and peace, especially in its own region. This was followed, in reaction, by a revival of nationalism in China itself. Although the China threat theory did not decisively influence the policies of Western governments, virtually all of which continued to pursue engagement with China, it did gain currency among academics and government officials and in parliaments and congresses, especially in the United States.

The institutions of a democratic China will probably evolve from the present structure. The system will probably have a single supreme legislature like the National People's Congress, unicameral and not subject to judicial review. It may have a single dominant party like those in Taiwan and Japan that stays in office permanently. This is most likely to be the Communist Party, because they will enter the democratizing transition with enormous advantages—size, organizational sophistication, control over resources—and will use them to fight and win elections. Protecting the vested interests of party members and party-chosen bureaucrats will be high on the agenda of the politicians who engineer the transition.

The factionalized opposition will probably develop out of the existing satellite parties as well as some exile democratic organizations acceptable to the communists. Elections will be short and hard-fought, with manifestoes and personal attacks, and will draw high participation rates, but many of the voters will be mobilized on the basis of personal ties to the candidates or payoffs from political machines rather than issues. Some broad version of socialism will continue to be the official ideology and few politicians will question it. The press, freed from government control, will be intensely partisan, with every journal serving the interests of some party, party faction, or social group. Readers will still have to read between the lines, and much of what they read will not be true. The military will continue to serve as a silent arbiter, its interventions kept as much as possible from the public eye, and will continue for a long time to owe its primary loyalty to the ruling party.

Although some of the exile democrats advocate that China adopt American-style federalism and separation of powers, I suspect that neither will be adopted because they are unfamiliar and would tend to divide power that will already be fragmented. China will continue to seek governmental efficiency through an ostensibly centralized system of undivided sovereignty. But the tug-of-war between the central government and provinces as big as European states will continue, and the center will probably weaken as the provinces prosper. . . .

Although many countries fear a strong China, a weak China is even more threatening because of the damage it can do to itself and to the world. From now on, it is doubtful that an undemocratic China can be stable and strong. A more democratic system may give China more real stability than the cycles of repression and popular outrage that have shaken the country throughout the twentieth century. To be sure, clashes of interest and personality that had been hidden would be visible, and no one would be in full control. But democratic institutions might provide peaceful and legitimate channels for resolving issues of power and policy, ways of forming a national consensus on important issues and of changing policies to serve it, a political environment that fosters economic growth, protection for dissent, and means for the political system to continue to evolve without mass violence.

THE FEAR OF CHINA

RICHARD BERNSTEIN AND ROSS MUNRO

Probably the most important work representing the China threat point of view was The Coming Conflict with China *by Richard Bernstein and Ross Munro, published early in 1997 within weeks of Deng Xiaoping's death. Richard Bernstein had been* Time *magazine's first Beijing bureau chief in 1980 and later moved to work for* The New York Times. *Canadian Munro headed the Foreign Policy Institute in Philadelphia at the time of the book's publication, but had worked with the American human rights organization Asiawatch and was in Beijing at the time of the 1989 crisis. Both had already written extensively about China, tending to adopt a highly critical and negative stance.*

I f China remains aggressive and the United States naïve, the looming conflict between the two countries could even lead to military hostilities. The United States, after all, has been in major wars in Asia three times in the past half century, always to prevent a single power from gaining ascendancy there, and there seems little question that China over the next decade or two will be ascendant on its side of the Pacific. But even without actual war, the rivalry between China and the United States will be the major global rivalry in the first decades of the twenty-first century, the rivalry that will force other countries to take sides and that will involve all of the major items of competition: military strength, economic well-being, influence among other nations and over the values and practices that are accepted as international norms.

74

CHINA IN DISARRAY

JAMES MILES

Views such as those of Bernstein and Munro veer heavily towards the pessimistic, but still do not predict great misery for the Chinese people. A scenario which sees not a powerful and united China but a country 'in disarray' has been predicted by James Miles, mentioned in Chapter 59. 'Tiananmen' is a reference to the suppression of the student movement in June 1989.

China is now facing the most uncertain period of its political life since the communists came to power. The death of Deng will mark the end of a leadership system dominated by veteran revolutionaries whose authority rests on careers dating from well before the communist takeover in 1949. Those fighting for power after Deng's death will be younger men in the main who played little if any role in the civil war that brought the communists to power. Deng's strength, like Mao Zedong's, has depended to a considerable extent on his credibility within the military, built up during his years as a guerrilla commander. Mao and Deng were able to control a country as large and diverse as China not least because there was mutual respect and understanding between themselves and professional soldiers. Deng's designated civilian successors have no combat experience.

It was lucky for the party and its leaders that Deng eventually managed to override the paralyzing factional disputes during Tiananmen. Without him, the crisis might have ended very differently. Deng himself has often warned that civil war might break out and millions of refugees pour across the country's borders if communist authority collapses. While such apocalyptic statements are, of course, aimed at frightening radical reformers into silence, they are not to be dismissed as mere propaganda.

Many Chinese, including many firebrand dissidents, see his point, as do many of China's neighbours.

When cracks begin to appear more openly in the political structure, as I believe they eventually will, the Pandora's box of rivalry, hatred, vengefulness, and a myriad other destructive emotions will spill open just as they did in some of the former communist countries of Eastern Europe and parts of the former Soviet Union. There are those who might argue that China has been through chaos before, during the Cultural Revolution and in 1989, for example, and has managed not only to reorganize but, in the end, to achieve astonishing growth. This, however, was achieved under the direction of powerful personalities such as Mao Zedong and Deng Xiaoping, who may have been responsible for creating the chaos in the first place but nonetheless had the strength to curb it when it threatened to spin out of control. What would happen if, as seems likely in the not-too-distant future, there is no one in the leadership with the political authority of Mao or Deng? Hong Kong and Taiwan—the latter being home to the only armed political opposition to the Communist Party—might find themselves sucked into the maelstrom. But the consequences of chaos would be felt all over the world.

The Chinese revolution that began in the twilight years of the Qing dynasty more than a century ago is still far from reaching its conclusion. For all its seeming familiarity with the modern ways of the capitalist West, China is a country saddled with enormous baggage from its past. The rapid economic growth of the last few years is by no means a guarantee that China has at last found the secret of cohesion, nor do Deng's hard-line critics offer any viable alternatives.

75

RISING EXPECTATIONS

LAURENCE BRAHM

*A much more optimistic view of China's near-future emerges from the
1996 book by Laurence Brahm, already quoted in Chapter 66. Brahm
writes exuberantly about the changes for the better he has seen in China
since he first visited the country in 1981. His focus is on the economy, but
he also includes political and social improvements.*

'There was a time in the 1980s when all of us Chinese would
have gone abroad if there was the chance,' reminisced
one modern Chinese artist in Beijing. 'Today, I think few
would do so without a guarantee of basic economic conditions
overseas. Who wants to struggle as a dishboy in a Chinatown
restaurant with all of the opportunities here in China today?'

The artist sells his paintings in China for US$500 each. 'You
know, I can easily get US$2000 each in Hong Kong; in America,
they sell my paintings for US$6500.' He laughs as he touches up
the edges of a picture of Mao pasted on the breast of a nude female
figure painted on his canvas. 'I can paint what I want.' He then
pastes Renminbi notes [the Chinese currency] onto the crotch of
the figure—unabashed symbolism—and laughs, 'I couldn't do this
a few years ago, but nobody cares now.'

The Western media seem to paint a different view. Corruption,
crime, loss of traditional values, intellectual property protection,
human rights—these subjects form the steady diet of Western
journalists, who focus on nothing but the endless 'problems of
China'. Despite this, there is a small but growing body of Western
journalists in China today who do not share this negativism. There
is an eerie parallel between the current situation and the
frustration of earlier journalists in World War II who found their
positive reporting of the Communists in Yan'an simply edited out
of the published news.

What developing nations do not have the problems that come with development? What developed nations do not have these or worse problems (racial strife, drug abuse, inner-city violence)? The debate is pointless. The point is that since introducing its economic reforms in 1979, China has made probably greater progress than any other country in reforming its economy and raising the standard of living of most of its people. On a drive through a desolate countryside 15 years ago, one would be greeted by wide-eyed hungry peasants squatting in the dust amidst a village of collapsing huts. The same drive today is along a superhighway, with orderly thriving farming communities, healthy children, and schools. . . .

There seems to be a fear in the West that China's growth will somehow transcend China's borders. Old fears dating from the McCarthy era and the domino theory of John Foster Dulles have become a kind of collective unconscious in America. Analysis of events in China seems to take place in a time warp which American policy-makers seem to be unable to break out of. A plethora of problems lies ahead of China which will need to be systematically addressed by its leadership; its leadership has its hands more than full with domestic concerns to even contemplate the kind of

The tradition of Zhouzhuang is especially appropriate for tourism. The locals have set up fine restaurants and shops selling the 'special products' of the town to the tourists. A group of tourists is shown wandering through the streets. Photograph by Colin Mackerras.

aggressive threat that might substantiate the West's fears of a past era. . . .

The West worries over what will happen after Deng Xiaoping passes from the scene; most Chinese do not worry or even think about this. In their minds, the new leadership is already on-stage and Deng, for all intents and purposes, is not there. While China's current leadership line-up may be old and tainted by the events of the past, it is those same events that give the leadership a clear vision of the future.

The question for China then is not what will happen to today's leadership, it is can the future generation growing up in a soon-to-be-affluent China have the same vision as today's leadership? Without experiencing a cultural revolution, or more simply the trials and pain of rebuilding an economy and managing tumultuous growth, will China's leaders of tomorrow have the instinctive ability to lead the economy to new heights?

Already much of the blasé arrogance which has long affected affluent youth in Europe, America and, more recently, Japan, has begun to seep into the latest generation of university graduates in China. They have witnessed the seemingly impossible that is China's growth of the past five years, and now take this growth for granted. The result is that the current generation of university graduates now expect everything at once. They sneer at the value called patience which was critical to some of the hard decisions made 10–15 years ago which have brought about the results we see today. They have not seen—and do not care—about the pain the current leadership suffered to make impossibility a reality. They have not worked for these results, and do not feel they have to. What will the next generation do with this reality? Will they know how to make the future work for China? In China today, many are sceptical and worry about this single question.

251

76

THE EMPIRE, LONG UNITED

CHRIS TAYLOR, ROBERT STOREY, NICKO GONCHAROFF,

ET AL.

The question of whether China would stay together as a united country came to the fore in the 1990s. Reasons for this development include the 1989 crisis and the troubles in minority areas, especially Tibet in the late 1980s and Xinjiang in 1990.

The following passage considers the possibility of a break-up to be reasonably high and presents a bleak overall view of China's near-future. It comes from the fifth edition of China: A Lonely Planet Travel Survival Kit, *which came out in 1996 and was compiled by Chris Taylor, Robert Storey, and others. The first edition was published in 1984 and all versions have proved popular and influential, especially among young people. Asians as well as Westerners use the guide, and a glance at the list of people who have offered advice shows they come from many countries. The authors— English, American, and Australian—make no pretence to be specialists on China, but they do claim good research and wide knowledge, and their views are taken seriously by their readers.*

Faced with a looming inner-Party power struggle and an overall situation of increasingly uneven economic development, both Chinese and foreign experts have begun to voice concerns that China might break up. It has become fashionable to quote the first paragraph of *Romance of the Three Kingdoms*, a classic novel that describes the struggles to reunify the empire during the Three Kingdoms period: 'The empire, long united, must divide; long divided, must unite. Thus it has always been.'

China's empires do indeed have a long tradition of breaking up, and the problems facing the current regime make it ripe for radical change if not total collapse. The problems that led to the protests and bloodshed of 1989 are still present: inflation is thought to be running at around 25 per cent and official corruption permeates the entire system despite occasional widely publicized drives to stamp it out. The central government meanwhile complains of increasing regional power—in particular the affluent coastal cities of Shanghai and Guangzhou—and has difficulties collecting the taxes it claims as its own. The state is also saddled with some 100,000 state-owned firms, of which at least half are thought to be losing money. Together they employ over 100 million workers; restructuring would result in massive layoffs and social dislocation.

Perhaps most dangerous of all, rural incomes have stagnated in recent years, leading to widespread social unrest: in 1993 alone 830 incidents of rural revolt involving crowds of over 500 were reported in the Chinese press.

If all this were not bad enough, China's looming grain crisis is truly disastrous. Desertification, industrialization, urbanization, and various energy projects have probably destroyed around a third of China's cropland over the last 40 years. This along with natural disasters, such as frequent flooding in southern China, probably means that China will become increasingly reliant on grain imports.

Ironically, however, if the Western press is not announcing the coming collapse of China (with its attendant consequences for the world economy), it is warning of the dangers of an ascending newly empowered China. Defence spending has been steadily on the rise in recent years and foreign sources currently place figures at anywhere between US$10 billion and US$50 billion annually. Both the USA and China's Asian neighbours are watching the situation closely.

The next few years will be critical for China. A smooth takeover of power in Hong Kong is essential, as is a smooth transition of power in the central government after the death of Deng. Restructuring of the economy has to continue if the government wants to deliver the affluent lifestyle that more and more Chinese are demanding as their right. And the central government will probably find itself under increasing pressure to provide greater freedoms and to undertake a degree of democratic reform. All or any of these could go wrong.

77

CHINA NEED NOT COLLAPSE

STEPHEN FITZGERALD

The following passage by Stephen FitzGerald is from a book published in Australia, a country not among those included in this book. Yet it expresses so thoughtful and rounded a summation of China's future that I have included it anyway.

C hinese politics is of course unstable. It could fall apart. The Chinese Communist Party has lost it, the Party itself and all it goes by in the way of ideological conformity, statewide control, 'commandism' from the centre. No one believes in it. The Party remains, but there is still nothing to put in its place. At the same time international communism is also laid bare in all its evils, and discredited. Even if someone wanted to reassert that kind of control in China, it could not do so because the Party is not now dealing with an exhausted, cowed, and desperately poor populace. We have to remember that the Party came to power in 1949 because the people turned to it for salvation. Few would do that now, although many are joining it as a path to position and preferment. And the Party in the old sense has lost its will. This does not mean that they don't try to control what people read and think, or put people in gaol, violate human rights every day, maintain files on everyone, and control intellectuals and political opponents. But China did all of that before the communists, and so did Taiwan until the 1970s, and so still to some extent do Korea and Singapore. Many Chinese in fact approved of the putting down of the demonstrations in Beijing in June 1989, and many of those I hear this from are in Taiwan and Singapore.

There is no doubt that China also has massive problems elsewhere, including regional disparities in wealth, a huge itinerant population, and the overwhelming burden of inefficient and insolvent state enterprises. There are, however, more factors in the equation which suggest that China is going to make it than there is evidence of eventual collapse, Soviet-style, and these include the following.

One is China's track record. It is now twenty years since Mao died, and there has been rather extraordinary effective economic and political management over the period. Extraordinary, because this has been management of change on a huge scale, management of a transition few others in history have confronted and from a tradition no other country has had to bear. They have managed—to take a few examples at random—the dismantling of communal agriculture and wholesale agricultural reform, the introduction of a modern education system, the dismantling of the irrational socialist pricing structure, the establishment of a realistic exchange rate, the opening of industry to foreign participation, the development of consumerism including department stores and chains selling made-outside-China goods direct to the Chinese consumer, the application to just about every part of China— including Tibet!—of special economic zone policies trialled with such success in Shenzhen, the employment-generating effects of investment from off-shore, and the policy that the free market rules (with a last nostalgic nod in the direction of Chairman Mao by calling it market socialism). All this, and much more.

And it has worked well enough for China to be a magnet for international investment. Two major and many minor political eruptions in the streets have neither brought the regime down nor turned it from its purpose. China is of course not democratic. But perhaps you have to have lived in China before to know just how open it is now, and how many people have a sense of freedom about their lives and their ability to come and go and do as they please.

A second factor has been the role of Chinese tycoons, at first from Hong Kong but later from Southeast Asia and Taiwan. Their knowledge and experience and advice has been and still is at the direct service of Chinese leaders, and has guided and will continue to guide the leadership through many difficult decisions of economic reform and liberalization in an informal and private way.

A third is the resumption of what might be called traditional Chinese politics. One part of this is the restoration in party and government of rule by great families and their extended connections and family alliances. Most Chinese of course prefer that government stay as far away from them as possible. However, they also recognize that it is a fact of life that governments almost by definition continually make trouble, not only through taxes and other impositions (hence the well-known and universal practice in Taiwan whereby every business has two sets of books), but by their internal disputes and conflicts, and civil wars and warlordism of the kind seen in the first half of this century. They have therefore learnt to accept political instability as an ever-imminent possibility, and to live with it and through it. They would never have made the mistake Western leaders made about the way in which the Chinese Government handled Tiananmen because they would not have expected otherwise. But the re-emergence of rule by great families ties government back into a very familiar relationship with society, and business, which everyone knows and feels more or less comfortable with. Chinese societies live by such connections, and their restoration at the top and throughout the provinces restores the networks which communicate and facilitate and cushion. The families which rule Beijing all have strong ties with business interests and tycoons, inside China, in Hong Kong and Macao and Southeast Asia, and in Taiwan.

Another feature of traditional Chinese politics is the general acceptance in such societies of what is called 'power distance', which accords rulers and leaders much greater freedom to pursue and enjoy power and its rewards than in English-speaking societies. Although this may change over time, for the foreseeable future it will mitigate the tensions between the haves in power and the have-nots. The Chinese Government understands that there is a limit to public tolerance of the use of office for personal gain, and applies brakes to keep it in acceptable bounds.

A fourth factor is that Chinese are almost by birth or instinct materialist. In Chinese society anywhere that is the hallmark. You have to have money to satisfy that instinct, and no people I know work harder at making money if they are allowed to keep it than Chinese. In that once purest of Marxist-Leninist countries, Chinese are now allowed to do both. Ideology is out. Getting rich is in. Unless you live next door to a jealous official who hasn't had the opportunity to line his pockets, there are no inhibitions on legitimately making money and getting rich. So the Chinese are now in their natural element, and revelling in it. Disposable incomes are rising. And so is the size of the middle class. In one sense—aspiration—every Chinese is born middle-class. In terms of more conventional measurements of what is middle-class, its size is already somewhere between 2 and 5 per cent of the total population, probably already around 30 million people and rising fast. These are concentrated in the southern and coastal provinces. Pursuit of the material, and getting rich, is a 'freedom'. This is now open to everyone to seek (even if they don't all find), and everyone in the political process is benefiting materially in some way or other. Many of course have their snouts deep in the trough. Every ministry and department and bureau and provincial government and research institute in China, and almost every one of the powerful personalities, has an office or corporation or some beneficial connection in Shenzhen, Hong Kong, or somewhere where the money action is, and many have children studying abroad. Political instability of any kind will be detrimental to these interests. But there are many more who benefit simply from companies in which they have a legitimate interest, or from the general rewards available to the middle class in a growth economy.

SINOPHILES AND SINOPHOBES

GEOFFREY MURRAY

The final extract, from Geoffrey Murray, an author cited earlier, sums up a reasonably impartial view about China's future from somebody who likes the Chinese despite their weaknesses. It is an appropriate passage to end this book for the way it sets China in a world context both historically and geographically.

In preparation for writing this book, I have spent considerable time in second-hand bookshops and libraries seeking a wide variety of writings on China from the nineteenth century up to the present day. And what is most striking is the strong emotions, for good or bad, that the Chinese seem to arouse in so many breasts. One either has to be a rabid anti-Communist, seeing a Chinese red devil under every bed, or one is at least a 'fellow traveller', seeing China as the promised land for every true Marxist, along the lines of 'I have seen the future and it works'. Whether a sinophile or a sinophobe, one is free to visit China and the likelihood is that one will see that particular view confirmed.

In the past, the Western choice of misconception of China and the Chinese seems to have depended on the individual's state of Christian devoutness or when one was born. From the agnostic of the eighteenth century comes the image of the great Confucian state moving majestically down the centuries, changeless, peaceful, inert, and practically embalmed beneath the rule of its godlike emperors and the government of the wisest scholars. To the Victorian churchgoer, on the other hand, China was the nightmare of the Protestant missionary, a godless kingdom of sinful rogues and heathens. It was, after all, pious horror at the behaviour of the benighted that first gave us the image of Dr Fu Manchu and his friends, the cultivated, callous opium-smoking criminal, all long knives. Then, there are the comic laundrymen, the ship's cook, the fat greasy restaurateurs, and the most inscrutable of all, the moon-faced Mao and his fanatical coterie of sycophants waving their Little Red Books in unison. Never perhaps have a single people been so subject to stereotypical vilification for so long.

Since 1990, I have spent much of my time living and working in China, and I believe I have seen both the best and the worst in the Chinese people. They are canny, pragmatic, hard-working, sensitive, often very excitable, and sometimes deplorably stupid. They can be cruelly indifferent as well as extremely warm-hearted; honest and cunning; open and close-mouthed. And I must admit that I happen to like them very much indeed. But whatever one's view is on China and the Chinese, neither can be ignored. Many pundits have expressed the view that global politics and the economy in the twenty-first century will focus on Pacific Asia. If true, the key fact is that the Chinese dragon, asleep for a century or so, is now awakening with a vengeance.

The economic reform and opening-up policies adopted by China since 1978 have led to profound and extensive changes in its politics, economy, society, and culture. The rapid rise of China's economy, its large population, strategic position and huge potential market, and its enhanced international status have made China's future development a key factor in post-Cold War world peace and order, the Oriental-Occidental cultural relationship, the North-South economic order and the Sino-US and the Sino-Japanese relationships.

From this emerged the perception that China is on the verge of becoming a Superpower, if it is not already one. The superpowers that have preceded it over the ages have all significantly shaped the world of their day, and China is unlikely to be any exception—especially given its vital geopolitical location, with the Muslim states of Central Asia on its western edge, the ailing but still powerful Russian bear to the north, the once booming (now temporarily wounded) economies of Southeast Asia on the southern rim, and the developed economic powerhouses of Japan and South Korea just a short sea journey away.

NOTES

Introduction

1. Frances Wood, *Did Marco Polo Go to China?*, London: Secker & Warburg, 1995, p. 150.
2. Richard Humble, *Marco Polo*, New York: G. P. Putnam's Sons, 1975, p. 35.
3. The notion of the pendulum theory has been challenged on the grounds that it does not fit the Australian experience over several decades of the twentieth century. See Lachlan Strahan, *Australia's China: Changing Perceptions from the 1930s to the 1990s*, New York: Cambridge University Press, 1996.

Part II
Chapter 4

1. C. R. Boxer, 'Introduction', in C. R. Boxer, ed., *South China in the Sixteenth Century, Being the Narratives of Galeote Pereira, Fr. Gaspar da Cruz, OP, Fr. Martín de Rada, O.E.S.A. (1559–1575)*, London: The Hakluyt Society, 1953; Nendeln/Liechtenstein: Kraus Reprint, 1967, p. xc.
2. Juan Gonzalez de Mendoza, *The History of the Great and Mighty Kingdom of China and The Situation Thereof*, translated by R. Parke, Sir George T. Staunton, Bart., ed., with an Introduction by R. H. Major, 2 Vols., London: The Hakluyt Society, 1853–4, Vol. I, p. 6.

Part IV
Chapter 7

1. The original French version gives a footnote with references to *Essai sur les moeurs et l'esprit des nations* and others of his own works.
2. The original French has Wolf.
3. The original French has Hall.
4. Voltaire, *Dictionnaire philosophique, dans lequel sont réunis les questions sur l'Encyclopédie, L'opinion en alphabet, les articles insérés dans*

l'Encyclopédie, et plusieurs destinés pour le dictionnnaire de l'Académie Française, etc., 14 Volumes, Paris: Didot, 1816, Vol. IV, pp. 256–7, 262–3, 264–5. I have followed the translation given in Voltaire, *A Philosophical Dictionary*, 2 Volumes, London: E. Truelove, 1843, Vol. I, pp. 265, 267–8, 268, where unfortunately no translator is acknowledged.

Chapter 9

1. On Lord Anson, see Part V.

Part VI
Chapter 14

1. Translation by Colin Mackerras. An alternative translation of a small portion of this passage, and of some of the sections missing here, which are of similar tenor, is given in J. A. G. Roberts, *China Through Western Eyes, The Nineteenth Century, A Reader in History*, United Kingdom: Alan Sutton, 1991, pp. 73–4.

Chapter 16

1. See, for instance, Colin Mackerras, *Western Images of China*, Hong Kong: Oxford University Press, 1989, pp. 48–9 and J. A. G. Roberts, *China Through Western Eyes, The Nineteenth Century, A Reader in History*, United Kingdom: Alan Sutton, 1991, pp. 147–8.

Part XI
Chapter 44

1. Harold R. Isaacs, *Images of Asia, American Views of China and India*, New York: Harper Torchbooks, 1972, p. xv.

Part XII
Chapter 49

1. John S. Service, 'Introduction', in Fredric M. Kaplan, Julian M. Sobin, and Stephen Andors, *Encyclopedia of China Today*, New York: Eurasia Press, Inc., London and Basingstoke: Macmillan, 1979, p. xv.

Part XIII
Chapter 58

1. Quoted from Simon Leys, 'After the Massacres', in George Hicks, ed., *The Broken Mirror: China After Tiananmen*, London: Longman Current Affairs, 1990, p. 160.

Chapter 62

1. Sheryl WuDunn, 'A Chinese Village Discovers the Road to Riches', *The New York Times*, 10 January 1992, p. A4.

Part XIV
Chapter 65

1. Seth Faison, 'Women as Chattel: In China, Slavery Rises', *The New York Times*, 6 September 1995, pp. A1, A10.

BIBLIOGRAPHY

Barrow, John, *Travels in China, Containing Descriptions, Observations, and Comparisons, Made and Collected in the Course of a Short Residence at the Imperial Palace of Yuen-min-yuen, and on a Subsequent Journey through the Country from Pekin to Canton, in which it is Attempted to Appreciate the Rank that this Extraordinary Empire May be Considered to Hold in the Scale of Civilized Nations,* second revised edition, London: T. Cadell and W. Davies, The Strand, 1806.

Baum, Richard, *Burying Mao, Chinese Politics in the Age of Deng Xiaoping,* Princeton: Princeton University Press, 1994.

Beresford, Lord Charles, *The Break-up of China, With an Account of its Present Commerce, Currency, Waterways, Armies, Railways, Politics and Future Prospects,* London: Harper & Brothers, 1899.

Bergère, Marie-Claire, *La République populaire de Chine de 1949 à nos jours,* Paris: Armand Colin, 1987.

Bernstein, Richard, *From the Center of the Earth, The Search for the Truth about China,* Boston: Little, Brown and Company, 1982.

Bernstein, Richard and Ross H. Munro, *The Coming Conflict with China,* New York: Alfred A. Knopf, 1997.

Blunden, Caroline and Mark Elvin, *The Cultural Atlas of the World, China,* Oxford: Phaidon, 1983; Oxford: Andromeda, Alexandria, Va.: Stonehenge, 1990.

Boxer, C. R., ed., *South China in the Sixteenth Century, Being the Narratives of Galeote Pereira, Fr. Gaspar da Cruz, OP, Fr. Martín de Rada, O.E.S.A. (1559–1575),* London: The Hakluyt Society, 1953; Nendeln/Liechtenstein: Kraus Reprint, 1967.

Brahm, Laurence J., *China as No 1, The New Superpower Takes Centre Stage,* Singapore: Butterworth-Heinemann Asia, 1996.

Broomhall, Marshall, *The Jubilee Story of the China Inland Mission,* London: Morgan & Scott, China Inland Mission, 1915.

Buck, Pearl S., *The Good Earth,* New York: John Day, 1931.

Buck, Pearl S., *My Several Worlds, A Personal Record,* New York: John Day, 1954

Butterfield, Fox, *China, Alive in the Bitter Sea,* London: Hodder and Stoughton, 1982.

Clayre, Alasdair, *The Heart of the Dragon*, London: Collins/Harvill, 1984.

Conger, Sarah Pike (Mrs E. H. Conger), *Letters from China With Particular Reference to the Empress Dowager and the Women of China*, Chicago: A. C. McClurg & Co., 1909.

Cradock, Percy, *Experiences of China*, London: John Murray, 1994.

Cranmer-Byng, J. L., edited, introduced, and annotated, *An Embassy to China, Being the Journal Kept by Lord Macartney during his Embassy to the Emperor Ch'ien-lung, 1793–1794*, London: Longmans, Green and Co., 1962.

Crow, Carl, drawings by G. Sapojnikoff, *Four Hundred Million Customers*, London: Hamish Hamilton, 1937.

Crow, Carl, *I Speak for the Chinese*, London: Hamish Hamilton, 1938.

Dietrich, Craig, *People's China, A Brief History*, (second ed.), New York: Oxford University Press, 1994.

Doolittle, Reverend Justus, *Social Life of the Chinese: With Some Account of their Religious, Governmental, Educational, and Business Customs and Opinions, with Special but not Exclusive Reference to Fuhchau*, (2 Vols.), Vol. II, New York: Harper & Brothers, 1865.

Doré, Henri, translated by M. Kennelly, SJ, *Researches into Chinese Superstitions*, (13 Vols.), Shanghai: T'usewei Printing Press, 1914.

Douglas, R. K., 'China', in *Encyclopædia Britannica, A Dictionary of Arts, Sciences, and General Literature*, ninth edition, (25 Vols.), Vol. V, Edinburgh: Adam and Charles Black, 1875–89.

Du Halde, Père J. B., translated by R. Brookes, *The General History of China Containing A Geographical, Historical, Chronological, Political and Physical Description of the Empire of China, Chinese-Tartary, Corea and Thibet. Including an Exact and Particular Account of their Customs, Manners, Ceremonies, Religion, Arts and Sciences*, (4 Vols.), Vol. II, London: John Watts, 1736.

Edmunds, Charles K., *Modern Education in China*, Washington, D. C.: Government Printing Office, 1919.

Feigon, Lee, *China Rising, The Meaning of Tiananmen*, Chicago: Ivan R. Dee, 1990.

FitzGerald, Stephen, *Is Australia an Asian Country? Can Australia Survive in an East Asian Future?*, Sydney: Allen & Unwin, 1997.

Gascoyne-Cecil, Reverend Lord William, assisted by Lady Florence Cecil, *Changing China*, New York: D. Appleton & Company, 1910.

Gilbert, Rodney, *What's Wrong with China*, London: John Murray, 1926.

Gittings, John, *Real China, From Cannibalism to Karaoke*, London: Simon & Schuster, 1996.

Gonzalez de Mendoza, Juan, translated by R. Parke, edited by Sir George T. Bart Staunton, with an Introduction by R. H. Major, *The History of the Great and Mighty Kingdom of China and The Situation Thereof*, (2 Vols.), Vol. I, London: The Hakluyt Society, 1853–4.

Gordon, Eric, *Freedom Is a Word*, London: Hodder and Stoughton, 1971.

Harding, Gardner L., *Present-Day China, A Narrative of a Nation's Advance*, New York: The Century Co., 1916.

Hicks, George, ed., *The Broken Mirror: China After Tiananmen*, London: Longman Current Affairs, 1990.

Huc, M. [Evariste Régis], *L'empire chinois, faisant suite a l'ouvrage intitulé Souvenirs d'un voyage dans la Tartarie et le Thibet*, (third ed.), (2 Vols.), Vol. I, Paris: Librairie de Gaume Frères, 1857.

Hudson, Christopher, ed., *The China Handbook*, Chicago, London: Fitzroy Dearborn Publishers, 1997.

Humble, Richard, *Marco Polo*, New York: G. P. Putnam's Sons, 1975.

Isaacs, Harold R., *Images of Asia, American Views of China and India*, New York: Harper Torchbooks, 1972.

Kaplan, Frederic M., Julian M. Sobin, and Stephen Andors, Introduction by John S. Service, *Encyclopedia of China Today*, New York: Eurasia Press, Inc; London: Macmillan, 1979.

Kraft, Joseph, *The Chinese Difference*, New York: Saturday Review Press, 1972.

Kristof, Nicholas D., and Sheryl WuDunn, *China Wakes, The Struggle for the Soul of a Rising Power*, New York: Vintage Books, Random House, 1995.

Legendre, A. F., translated by Elsie Martin Jones, *Modern Chinese Civilization*, London: Jonathan Cape, original introduction dated July 1926, preface to the English edition dated 28 August 1928, reprinted by Ch'eng Wen Publishing Company, Taipei, 1971.

Leys, Simon, *Les habits neufs du président Mao, Chronique de la 'Revolution culturelle'*, Paris: Éditions Champ Libre, 1971.

Leys, Simon, *Ombres Chinoises*, Paris: Union Générale d'Editions, 1974; *Chinese Shadows*, New York: The Viking Press, 1977.

Mackerras, Colin, *Western Images of China*, Hong Kong: Oxford University Press, 1989.

Marcuse, Jacques, *The Peking Papers, Leaves from the Notebook of a China Correspondent,* New York: E. P. Dutton & Co., 1967.

Martin, W. A. P., *A Cycle of Cathay, or China, South and North, with Personal Reminiscences,* New York: Fleming H. Revell Company, 1900.

Maugham, W. Somerset, *On a Chinese Screen,* New York: George H. Doran, 1922.

Meadows, Thomas Taylor, *The Chinese and their Rebellions, viewed in connection with Their National Philosophy, Ethics, Legislation, and Administration, to which is added, An Essay on Civilisation and Its Present State in the East and West,* London: Smith, Elder & Co., 1856.

Miles, James A. R., *The Legacy of Tiananmen, China in Disarray,* Ann Arbor: The University of Michigan Press, 1996.

Montesquieu, translated and edited by Anne M. Cohler, Basia Carolyn Miller, and Harold Samuel Stone, *The Spirit of the Laws,* Cambridge: Cambridge University Press, 1989.

Murray, Geoffrey, *China, The Next Superpower: Dilemmas in Change and Continuity,* Richmond, Surrey: China Library, Curzon Press, 1998.

Nathan, Andrew J., *China's Crisis, Dilemmas of Reform and Prospects for Democracy,* New York: Columbia University Press, 1990.

New York Times, The. (10 January 1992, p. A4; 6 September 1995, p. A1, A10.)

Oksenberg, Michel C., Michael D. Swaine and Daniel C. Lynch, *The Chinese Future,* Pacific Council on International Policy, Los Angeles, and Rand Center for Asia-Pacific Policy, Santa Monica, 1997.

Polo, Marco and Thomas Wright, (ed.), *The Travels of Marco Polo, The Venetian, The Translation of Marsden Revised, With a Selection of His Notes,* London: Henry G. Bohn, 1854.

Powell, John B., *My Twenty-five Years in China,* New York: The Macmillan Company, 1945.

Quesnay, François, 'Despotisme de la Chine' (March to June 1767), in *Œuvres économiques et philosophiques de F. Quesnay, fondateur du système physiocratique,* New York: Burt Franklin, 1888, reprinted 1969.

Rasmussen, O. D., *What's Right with China,* Shanghai: Commercial Press, 1928.

Ricci, Matteo, translated by Father Louis Gallagher, *China in the Sixteenth Century: The Journals of Matthew Ricci: 1583–1610*, New York: Random House, 1942, 1953.

Roberts, J. A. G., *China Through Western Eyes, The Nineteenth Century, A Reader in History*, United Kingdom: Alan Sutton, 1991.

Rohwer, Jim, *Asia Rising: How History's Biggest Middle Class Will Change the World*, London: Nicholas Brealey Publishing, 1996; Singapore: Butterworth-Heinemann Asia, 1995.

Salisbury, Harrison E., *The New Emperors, China in the Era of Mao and Deng*, Boston: Little, Brown and Company, 1992.

Salisbury, Harrison E., *To Peking—and Beyond, A Report on the New Asia*, New York: Quadrangle/The New York Times Book Co., 1973.

Smedley, Agnes, *China's Red Army Marches*, London: Lawrence and Wishart, 1936

Smith, Adam, *An Inquiry into the Nature and Causes of the Wealth of Nations*, (2 Vols.), Vol. I, London: The World Classics, Grant Richards, 1904.

Smith, A. H., *Chinese Characteristics*, (fifth ed.), Edinburgh: Oliphant Anderson and Ferrier, 1900.

Snow, Edgar, *Red Star Over China*, first revised and enlarged edition, New York: Grove Press, 1968.

Snow, Edgar, *The Long Revolution*, New York: Random House, 1972; also published as *China's Long Revolution*, Harmondsworth: Penguin, 1974

Strahan, Lachlan, *Australia's China: Changing Perceptions from the 1930s to the 1990s*, New York: Cambridge University Press, 1996.

Taylor, Chris, Robert Storey and Nicko Goncharoff, a.o., *China A Lonely Planet Travel Survival Kit*, (fifth ed.), Melbourne: Lonely Planet Publications, 1996.

Toynbee, Arnold J., *A Journey to China or Things Which Are Seen*, London: Constable and Co., 1931; Westport, Connecticut: Hyperion Press reprint, 1977.

Voltaire, *Dictionnaire philosophique, dans lequel sont réunis les questions sur l'Encyclopédie, L'opinion en alphabet, les articles insérés dans l'Encyclopédie, et plusieurs destinés pour le dictionnnaire de l'Académie Française, etc.*, (14 Vols.), Vol. IV, Paris: Didot, 1816.

Voltaire, *Essai sur les moeurs et l'esprit des nations, et sur les principaux faits de l'histoire depuis Charlemagne jusqu'à Louis XIII*, 8 Vols., Vol. VIII, Paris: Didot, 1817.

Voltaire, *A Philosophical Dictionary*, (2 Vols.), Vol. I, London: E. Truelove, 1843.

Voltaire, *The Philosophy of History*, with a Preface by Thomas Kiernan, New York: The Citadel Press, 1965, a reprint of the original edition of 1766.

Voltaire, *Tchao chi cou ell*: or *The Little Orphan of the Family of Tchao. A Chinese Tragedy*, in Père J. B. Du Halde, *The General History of China* (4 Vols.), Vol. III, translated by R. Brookes, London: John Watts, 1736.

Walter, Richard and Benjamin Robins, edited with an Introduction by Glyndwr Williams, *A Voyage round the World in the Years MDCCXL, I, II, III, IV by George Anson*, London: Oxford University Press, 1974.

Williams, S. Wells, *The Middle Kingdom, A Survey of the Geography, Government, Literature, Social Life, Arts, and History of the Chinese Empire and Its Inhabitants*, (2 Vols.), Vol. I, revised edition, New York: Charles Scribner's Sons, 1883.

Wood, Frances, *Did Marco Polo Go to China?*, London: Secker & Warburg, 1995.

Wright, Elizabeth, *The Chinese People Stand Up*, London: BBC Books, 1989.

Yule, Colonel Sir Henry and Henri Cordier, *Cathay and the Way Thither, Being a Collection of Medieval Notices of China*, (4 Vols.), Vol. II, London: The Hakluyt Society, 1913–16.